NEW OXFORD ENGLISH SERIES
General Editor A. NORMAN JEFFARES

MATTHEW ARNOLD. F. W. Watt
BYRON. T. J. B. Spencer
COLERIDGE. J. A. Colmer
COWPER. A. Norman Jeffares
DRYDEN. J. Kinsley
G. M. HOPKINS. G. Storey
KEATS. R. Sharrock
POPE. D. Grant
SHELLEY. G. M. Matthews
SPENSER. J. F. Kermode
TENNYSON. Michael Millgate
WORDSWORTH. John Butt

NEW OXFORD ENGLISH SERIES

General Editor: A. NORMAN JEFFARES

SHELLEY

SELECTED POEMS AND PROSE

Chosen and edited by

G. M. MATTHEWS

LECTURER IN ENGLISH LITERATURE
UNIVERSITY OF LEEDS

OXFORD UNIVERSITY PRESS

1964

Oxford University Press, Amen House, London E.C.4

GLASGOW NEW YORK TORONTO MELBOURNE WELLINGTON
BOMBAY CALCUTTA MADRAS KARACHI LAHORE DACCA
CAPE TOWN SALISBURY NAIROBI IBADAN ACCRA
KUALA LUMPUR HONG KONG

Printed in Great Britain by
The Camelot Press Ltd., London and Southampton

ACKNOWLEDGMENTS

ALL the poems in this selection have been re-edited. I am grateful to the Trustees of the British Museum for permission to base the text of *The Mask of Anarchy* on the manuscript in the Ashley Collection; to the University Library, Cambridge, for *To Jane. The Invitation*; to the Delegates of the Clarendon Press for *England in 1819*, *The Pursued and the Pursuer*, *Apollo Sings*, *The Aziola*, *The Triumph of Life*, and *Lines written in the Bay of Lerici*; to the Provost and Fellows of Eton College for *Love's Philosophy*; and to the Harvard College Library for *Song*. The following kindly allowed manuscripts to be used in collation: The William Luther Lewis Collection of Rare Books and Manuscripts in The Mary Couts Burnett Library, Texas Christian University, Fort Worth, Texas; the Delegates of the Clarendon Press; The Harvard College Library; The Huntington Library, San Marino, California; and The Pierpont Morgan Library.

I am indebted to the Oxford University Press, to the Syndics of the Cambridge University Press, to Messrs. Macmillan & Co., to the University of North Carolina Press, to the Edinburgh University Press, to The Public Trustee and the Society of Authors, to Messrs. Heinemann, to the Harvard University Press, and to Penguin Books Ltd., for permission to reprint the quotations on pp. 30, 31, 32-33, 34, 35-36, 39, 41-42, 43, and 213 respectively.

I should like also to thank Dr. David C. Mearns, Chief of the Manuscript Division, Library of Congress; the staff of the Bodleian Library; Dr. H. K. Prescot, Librarian of Eton College; Professor H. W. Donner, editor of

Studia Neophilologica; Mr. Jon Silkin, editor of *Stand*; and Professor David B. Owens for so generously sharing his knowledge.

G.M.M.

April 1963

CONTENTS

INTRODUCTION

PERCY BYSSHE SHELLEY was born on 4 August 1792 into a family of country gentry that had very recently come into money, and acquired a baronetcy only in 1806. The poet's grandfather, Bysshe Shelley (born in America, of an American mother), had eloped with two rich heiresses in succession. His first wife was the poet's grandmother; his second was a Sidney, thus allowing Shelley to claim alliance with Sir Philip. These circumstances gave him some connexion with the newly-rich as well as with the high-born section of the upper class, though he soon repudiated both as 'the groveling sons of commerce and aristocracy'. His father ('that mistaken man'), who inherited the new baronetcy in 1815, lived at Field Place, a large country house near Horsham in Sussex. Shelley was the eldest child, with four sisters for playmates (he was already 13 when a brother, John, was born), so his departure at 10 for boarding-school, first at Syon House Academy in London, and then (1804) at Eton, meant a harsh change for one who had been the high-spirited leader of a family of girls. 'His imagination was always roving upon something romantic and extraordinary', wrote a Syon House contemporary,

such as spirits, fairies, fighting, volcanoes, &c., and he not unfrequently astonished his schoolfellows by blowing up the boundary palings of the playground with gunpowder, also the lid of his desk in the middle of schooltime . . .

These odd interests and escapades, combined with an excitable temper, invited cruel teasing. At Eton he was just as unconventional, and his torment was worse:

I have seen him surrounded, hooted, baited like a maddened bull,—
and at this distance of time I seem to hear ringing in my ears the cry
which Shelley was wont to utter in his paroxysm of revengeful
anger.

Perhaps such experiences suggested the images of hunted
creatures in Shelley's poetry; but the 'maddened bull' indi-
cates something less often recognized: a formidable fighting
impulse, which when roused he did not find easy to control.

Resistance to the abuses of public-school life came to a
crisis, probably at Eton, in a deliberate act of self-dedication,
a vow to be 'wise, and just, and free, and mild' in the face of
all arbitrary power:

> And from that hour did I with earnest thought
> Heap knowledge from forbidden mines of lore,
> Yet nothing that my tyrants knew or taught
> I cared to learn, but from that secret store
> Wrought linkèd armour for my soul, before
> It might walk forth to war among mankind . . .
> (Dedication to *The Revolt of Islam*, 1818)

The forbidden lore very likely included Godwin's anarchistic
Enquiry Concerning Political Justice (1793), and certainly
included science, not then taught at Eton. Astronomy,
chemistry, physics, fascinated him; his alarmed little sisters
'were placed hand-in-hand round the nursery table to be
electrified'. Also, like Wordsworth, he had an adolescent
craze for 'Death-demons, and skeletons dripping with the
putrefaction of the grave', which produced two 'Gothic'
novels—one written at school—and some bad poetry; but
gradually this sensational element was modified until in his
mature writing it finds a useful function, for instance in the
torture-scene of *Prometheus Unbound*, and in parts of *Adonais*.

Despite his earlier ordeals, Shelley had many friends at

Eton when, at 18, he went up to University College, Oxford, and met Thomas Jefferson Hogg, son of a Stockton landowner. The outcome of their arguments about God and society was a 950-word joint memorandum, *The Necessity of Atheism*. This asserted only that God's existence is not provable and was written to stimulate controversy, which they rashly made sure of doing by sending copies to the Bishops and to the Heads of Colleges, who were all clergymen. Shelley could neither admit nor deny authorship without implicating Hogg, and both were expelled for 'contumaciously refusing to answer questions proposed to them' by their College authorities.

Shelley felt persecuted; his boyhood engagement to a pretty cousin had already been broken off because of 'the tone of his letters on speculative subjects'. When Harriet Westbrook, a very attractive school friend of his sister's, complained of being victimized on account of her friendship with him, he 'advised her to resist', and finally eloped with her in August 1811. He was then just 19, she just 16. It was, he wrote later, a 'rash & heartless union'. Although he regarded marriage as a 'most despotic, most unrequired fetter', he married her because he thought that if they simply lived together the social disgrace would bear unfairly on her. But he was genuinely fond of her, and their fathers finally granted them an allowance, though not enough for incessant travel and the other commitments Shelley entered into, for he always gave away more than he spent—indeed, more than he owned. He taught Harriet Latin, and she tried to enter into his social and political activities, which included land reclamation on the Welsh coast, and two propaganda expeditions to Ireland. His major work of this period, *Queen Mab*, was dedicated to and inspired by her, the artfully innocent title masking a poem which he described as being 'in the most furious style, with long notes against Jesus Christ, God the Father, and the king, and the Bishops, and marriage, and the Devil knows what.'

From the birth in June 1813 of Ianthe, named after the heroine of *Queen Mab*, their differing interests and capabilities drew them apart. 'The partner of my life', Shelley told his friend Peacock, 'should be one who can feel poetry and understand philosophy.' Mary Godwin, 16-year-old daughter of the Radical philosopher William Godwin and of Mary Wollstonecraft, author of *A Vindication of the Rights of Woman*, seemed to respond to his needs. They fell passionately in love; and on 28 July 1814 (Mary's father having energetically declined to stand by his published views on relations between the sexes) they left secretly together for the Continent, taking with them as interpreter Claire Clairmont, daughter of the second Mrs. Godwin by her former husband. Their route led them through country devastated by the recent Napoleonic war. Shortage of funds hurried them back to England in mid-September, where the next nine months were miserably spent in efforts to borrow money (for Godwin as well as themselves), and in periods of enforced separation while Shelley hid from creditors. Mary's baby, born prematurely in February 1815, died within a fortnight. Not until June, when the death of his grandfather provided Shelley with an annuity of £1,000 (£200 of which he set aside annually for Harriet), were they able to settle at Bishopsgate, near Windsor. A ten-day voyage up the Thames improved his health and led to his first important poem for two years, *Alastor*, which depicts, and criticizes, a poet's solitary pursuit of an ideal love.

In May 1816 the Shelley household, now including a 4-month-old son William, set out again for Switzerland, and spent the summer on the Lake of Geneva near Byron—partly because Claire was having a love-affair with him. The *Hymn to Intellectual Beauty* and *Mont Blanc* were written in Switzerland. The two poets—Byron's work already famous, Shelley's almost unknown, but both men execrated as monsters of immorality—were mutually impressed, and for Shelley Byron remained the supreme creative personality of the age.

After their return that autumn two major tragedies occurred. Fanny Imlay, the odd girl out in Godwin's complicated family (she was Mary's illegitimate half-sister), committed suicide; and two months later, on 10 December, Shelley's wife Harriet, who may have got into bad company, was found drowned in the Serpentine. According to Leigh Hunt, whose friendship at this time was Shelley's chief comfort, Harriet's death 'tore his being to pieces', and its shadow undoubtedly affected the rest of his life.

To strengthen his claim on Harriet's children, Ianthe, and Charles (born after the separation), Shelley married Mary Godwin. But Lord Eldon refused in Chancery to allow him their custody, on the ground of immoral conduct. Shelley, who was fond of children, never forgot this judgement, and never lost his determination to get them back. Another complication was the birth, on 12 January 1817, of Allegra, daughter of Claire and Byron. Mary disliked living with Claire, rather resenting Shelley's affection for her, but for the time being there was no other way out.

The Shelleys now settled beside the Thames at Marlow, and the summer of 1817 was taken up not only by 'tea, Greek, and pedestrianism' in the company of Hogg, Peacock, or the Hunts, but by a major poem, probably begun in friendly rivalry with Keats's *Endymion*. Shelley's life at Marlow, however, where the post-war economic crisis had caused great suffering, was not one of poetic isolation:

He was up early; breakfasted sparingly; wrote this *Revolt of Islam* all the morning; went out in his boat or into the woods with some Greek author or the *Bible* in his hands; came home to a dinner of vegetables (for he took neither meat nor wine); visited (if necessary) '*the sick and the fatherless*,' whom others gave Bibles to and no help; wrote or studied again, or read to his wife and friends the whole evening; took a crust of bread or a glass of whey for his supper; and went early to bed. This is literally the whole of the life he led. . . .[1]

Unluckily the poem that under the title *Laon and Cythna* was to have startled readers out of their conventional ways of thinking also startled Shelley's publisher, and had to be toned-down, appearing finally in January 1818 as *The Revolt of Islam*.

Three months later for various reasons, including mildew, ill-health, and the problem of Allegra, the household left England for 'the Paradise of exiles, Italy'. The passage of the Alps, 'vast rifts and caverns in the granite precipices, wintry mountains with ice and snow above' and with the miserable subjects of the King of Sardinia below, suggested the setting of *Prometheus Unbound* Act I, begun that autumn. Soon after their arrival in Italy Allegra was sent to Byron at Venice, but Claire missed her so much that in August Shelley went to Venice to negotiate for the child to revisit her mother. His rides with Byron on the Lido, the sandbank fronting Venice, are commemorated in *Julian and Maddalo*, completed the following year. But in helping Claire with her daughter, Shelley lost his own: little Clara was soon buried on the same Lido, having died as a result of Mary's hasty journey to rejoin her husband.

In December 1818 the Shelleys explored Naples, the Bay of Baiae, Vesuvius, Pompeii—the volcanic region that suggested the realm of Demogorgon in *Prometheus Unbound* Act II, and

[1] Leigh Hunt, *The Examiner*, 10 October 1819.

the third stanza of the *Ode to the West Wind*: scenery 'more delightful than any within the immediate reach of civilized man'. From Naples they turned back to Rome, where in March and April 1819 Acts II and III of *Prometheus* were written amid the flower-overgrown ruins of the ancient city. *Prometheus Unbound* was the first of an astonishing series of achievements in verse and prose that runs right through the year 1819, despite the death in Rome of 3-year-old William on 7 June. 'How heavy a weight when misfortune is added to exile', Shelley wrote to Peacock of this second bitter blow, 'and solitude, as if the measure were not full, heaped high on both.'

Shelley always wrote best, however, when his personal suffering could be acted out in pity and indignation for others, and the news from England made this only too possible. Under the Speenhamland system of converting wages into poor-relief, agriculture was withering (so the *Edinburgh Review* put it) as if struck by a judgement from Heaven, while the unrest caused by an industrial slump was being mercilessly stamped down. Revolution seemed not unlikely. Near Leghorn, where the Shelleys had sought refuge from their 'Roman misery', *The Cenci* had been completed during the summer; here too, in the September after Peterloo, *The Mask of Anarchy* and a number of political songs and ballads were written which even Leigh Hunt dared not publish; and in Florence later that autumn Shelley wrote a 'party squib', *Peter Bell the Third*, aimed at the renegade Wordsworth; the carefully-reasoned political essay *A Philosophical View of Reform* and the mocking treatise *On the Devil and Devils*, both in prose; a lyrical epilogue to *Prometheus Unbound*; and the *Ode to the West Wind*. While at Naples Shelley had vainly tried to make up for Clara's death by 'adopting' an Italian baby (which also died the following year); now at last on 12

November 1819, 'after five hideous childless months', Mary Shelley's grief was relieved a little by the birth of another son, Percy Florence, who was to survive his father.

Early in 1820 the Shelleys moved to Pisa, and began for the first time to enjoy something like a social life. Shelley studied Spanish with Maria Gisborne, an old friend of Godwin's; Edward Williams and his wife Jane settled near by in January 1821; and Trelawny came in 1822—a young adventurer whose friendship was a great deal more genuine than his boasted career as a pirate has proved to be. Williams ('Melchior' in *The Boat on the Serchio*), an ex-cavalry officer from India, was liberal-minded, modest, capable: a first-rate sailing companion. Shelley's writings in 1820 included *The Witch of Atlas*, a long holiday-poem written in three days; an *Ode to Naples*, hailing the July insurrection in that city against King Ferdinand; and *Oedipus Tyrannus, or Swellfoot the Tyrant*, a dramatic skit on the public trial of Queen Caroline for immorality then proceeding in England. Late the same year he was introduced to an Italian girl, Emilia Viviani, who was confined by her parents in a convent, and his idealization of her had resulted by February 1821 in the most Platonic of his longer poems, *Epipsychidion* ('little companion-soul'). Disillusion soon followed, however, with both the girl and the poem.

Immediately after the arrival of the Williamses, an article attacking modern poetry by Peacock goaded Shelley into writing *A Defence of Poetry*. Then in mid-April came news that Keats had died in Rome, supposedly the victim of Tory reviewers. In *Adonais* Shelley could say, with the force of this immediate example, some of what he had just been saying in prose.

The death of Allegra in April 1822 made it essential to get Claire well away from Byron, whom she now hated, before the news reached her. Within a week, the Shelleys and the Williamses were sharing a house, Casa Magni, on the extreme sea-edge in the bay of Spezzia. This coast was then remote and beautiful; the sea came right up to the house front, so that in time of storm, Mary Shelley said, 'we almost fancied ourselves on board ship'. Shelley was happy there, and happier still when his new yacht, the *Don Juan*, arrived on 12 May. 'Williams is captain, and we drive along this delightful bay in the evening wind, under the summer moon, until earth appears another world. Jane brings her guitar, and if the past and the future could be obliterated, the present would content me so well that I could say with Faust to the passing moment, "Remain, thou, thou art so beautiful." ' The guitar had been a present from Shelley given with the poem beginning 'Ariel to Miranda'.

Mary, however, who had had a dangerous miscarriage, detested the place, and the beauty of the woods made her 'weep & shudder'. She hated sharing the housekeeping, difficult enough already in such isolation, with Jane Williams, obscurely aware of the attraction developing between her and Shelley. A heat-wave set in; the emotional tension, too, grew so unbearable that Shelley and Jane both began having hallucinations. It seemed to Shelley that he had reached a crisis in his life. He was nearly 30. The political 'winter of the world' was still unbroken; Peterloo had led only to further repression, and the revolution in Naples had been savagely put down by foreign troops. He was estranged from Mary and strongly drawn to the wife of one of his two best friends. His poetry, he thought, was disregarded or despised; he had thrown aside *Charles the First* unfinished, his last bid for dramatic success. What was he to do? His problems seemed insoluble, and writing *The Triumph of Life* did not solve them.

Then Leigh Hunt arrived in Italy to plan a new journal,

The Liberal: Verse and Prose from the South, with Byron and Shelley. Shelley sailed with Williams to welcome him at Leghorn, and started back on 8 July. The weather was uncertain and Shelley would have waited longer, but Williams was fretting at his long separation from Jane. Two hours out of Leghorn the *Don Juan* headed into a thunder-squall, and vanished.

Eight days later, Williams's body was washed ashore; and Shelley's soon after near Viareggio, with that of their young deck-hand. The local quarantine laws, which forbade normal burial, made their funeral ceremonies the most famous in English literary history. Disinterred from temporary graves in the sand, their bodies were burned on the seashore in an iron furnace, with pagan honours, under Trelawny's supervision:

. . . more wine was poured over Shelley's dead body than he had consumed during his life. This with the oil and salt made the yellow flames glisten and quiver. The heat from the sun and fire was so intense that the atmosphere was tremulous and wavy. The corpse fell open and the heart was laid bare. . . . Byron could not face this scene, he withdrew to the beach and swam off to the *Bolivar*. Leigh Hunt remained in the carriage.[1]

Shelley's ashes were buried in January 1823 near the pyramid of Cestius in Rome. It had been a short life. The ashes of Trelawny, who was born in the same year, were not laid beside his for another fifty-eight years.

Shelley need not now be regarded as either angelic or psychologically abnormal. In physique he was tall and slight, 'stag-eyed' and with a fresh complexion, which made him look extraordinarily young, although his thick brown hair was going grey before he died. All his life he suffered from

[1] *Trelawny's Recollections of the Last Days of Shelley and Byron*, ed. Dowden (London, 1923), p. 89.

pain in the side, perhaps organic but at least partly 'psycho-somatic', as it always grew worse when he was worried or unhappy. During his last summer he wrote that he was enjoying 'for the first time these ten years something like health . . . I find however that I must neither think nor feel, or the pain returns to its old nest'.

Leigh Hunt's eldest son described his features as firm and energetic, but 'an habitual eagerness of mood, thrusting forward his face, made him stoop, with sunken chest and rounded shoulders'—a posture encouraged by over-intense study. In his general build 'you saw well enough the indications of a masculine vigor, in many respects far above the average'. Nervous fatigue, or dejection, could quickly overcome him; physically he was tireless. A powerful walker, he would cover the 64 miles from Marlow to London and back in two days, spending one active day in town in between. 'His chief delight', wrote Hogg ruefully, 'was to walk at the rate of five miles an hour straight on end as long as it was light.' The work he put into composition was just as strenuous. Once when Trelawny found him writing he could only read the first two lines of the manuscript:

It was a frightful scrawl; words smeared out with his finger, and one upon the other, over and over in tiers, and all run together in most 'admired disorder'; it might have been taken for a sketch of a marsh overgrown with bulrushes, and the blots for wild ducks. . . . On my observing this to him he answered: 'When my brain gets heated with thought, it soon boils, and throws off images and words faster than I can skim them off. In the morning, when cooled down, out of the rude sketch as you justly call it, I shall attempt a drawing.'[1]

Most of Shelley's rough drafts look like that. The first stanza of the chorus from *Hellas* on page 152 takes up eight-and-a-half notebook pages, and is not even then in its final form.

---

[1] *Trelawny's Recollections*, pp. 49–50.

The 'invisible influence' of inspiration began the creative process, but the full powers of the mind were needed in order to carry it through: 'Poetry, although its source is native and involuntary, requires in its development severe attention.' *Prometheus Unbound*, Shelley said, cost him 'severe mental labour'.

Activity, incessant movement, characterized his life as it fills his poetry. 'He comes and goes like a spirit, no one knows when or where,' Trelawny was told on first meeting him. Indeed his friends made a standing joke of his journeys into Ireland, Scotland, Wales, and on the Continent, not to mention mere changes of address. When I praise the comforts of home, he wrote to Peacock from Switzerland, 'will you not liken me to Julius Caesar dedicating a temple to Liberty?' Water was his passion; he liked to escape 'to the nearest lake, river, or seashore, and only returned to roost at night'. Though often in danger, he could not swim, so that his various references to drowning are not surprising. What increased the risk was his fearlessness, which impressed Byron as well as Trelawny, both of them expert judges of physical courage. Once he gripped the locker-handles on a boat thought to be sinking, 'as cool as it was possible to be', in order to go down with the boat and so prevent Byron from risking his own life in trying to save him.

Impetuousness combined with activity and courage in Shelley's make-up. When his Italian doctor recommended either sailing or riding, he chose sailing, having, he said, 'enough to do in taming his own will, without the additional burthen of regulating that of a horse'. One adequate motive decided his course of action, after which 'nothing could make him pause for an instant when he had an object in view, until he had attained it'. His poems are written out in the same way, each line running bold and straight to the very edge of the paper, the last word then turning downward only if it must.

No one familiar with Shelley over his whole range could find him humourless. No other English poet is described by his friends as laughing so often and so heartily. Williams found him 'full of life and fun' in 1821; his cousin Medwin, who knew him both as a boy and at Pisa, said he was 'naturally full of playfulness . . . I have never met with anyone in whom the brilliance of wit and humour was more conspicuous'; and during his last days on earth, Hunt remembered making him laugh so much at a joke 'that he was obliged to lean against the passage of the Hotel, & beg me to desist'. Yet Hogg spoke of his 'strong aversion for laughter and ridicule'. In fact Shelley thought ridicule an evasion of responsibility: it was easier to laugh at something wrong than try to put it right. His gaiety was active and participating, not detached and malicious; he liked play-acting (once, disguised and in Sussex dialect, he got himself a job as gamekeeper's boy to a landed neighbour), and would act over his own jokes afterwards. This propensity, plus an excitable imagination, could sometimes lead to what Peacock called 'semi-delusions': invented or dressed-up incidents which he convinced himself had really happened. What Shelley had in abundance was not, perhaps, humour—contemplative enjoyment of human weakness—so much as fun, a high-spirited readiness to take on a role of mischief, which might be wry, ironical, or self-mocking. Fun of this kind created poems such as the *Letter to the Gisbornes* and *Peter Bell the Third*; it is close beneath the surface of lyrics like *The Cloud*, *The Pursued and the Pursuer*, and many others, and is not entirely absent from *The Indian Serenade*.

IDEAS AND BELIEFS

It is difficult to try to summarize Shelley's 'beliefs'. Like everyone else's, they developed with his experience, and even where they remained constant, his subtle-mindedness causes differing interpretations of the same evidence. Also, he was a poet, not a philosopher, and did not necessarily 'believe in' Reincarnation or the Ptolemaic system just because he sometimes made poetry out of these ideas. Yet in Shelley, for whom poets were the trumpets which sing to battle, the poetry cannot easily be disengaged from the deep convictions informing it.

Nature

Shelley said his chief pleasure in life was 'the contemplation of nature', and the poetry bears this out. Nature to him meant the cosmic environment and the great elemental processes: geological and seasonal change, storms, the water-cycle, volcanic activity, life and death. These processes, beautiful and terrible, were independent of man's activity. Yet human history was a continuation of cosmic history, and society was subject to the laws of change like all other objects and forms of life. The persistent image of *weaving* in Shelley's verse, with the many words allied to *inwoven: inwrought, entwining, implicated,* can help to convey this sense of universal interdependence.

His delight in the sun, on which he thought his health depended, and in the life created by it, made the seasons an inevitable symbol of the political and moral condition of mankind (see Appendix A). But the seasonal metaphor works both ways: if Spring comes, can Winter be far behind? Shelley recognized that history developed in phases of 'disorganization and reproduction', like the seasons and everything else in Nature. The reproductive half of the cycle, however, was unlikely to be shorter than the other half, which according to Prometheus had lasted 3,000 years; and in any case an evil could not be tolerated just because, if it

were removed, new 'riddles of death' (such as over-population) might crop up in sixty centuries' time. Besides, he
foresaw that science, its eyes unbanded after Jupiter's down-
fall to probe deeper into Nature's laws, would eventually
extend human control over the physical as well as the social
environment, and eliminate winter permanently in both.

Nature's cruelty, being independent of human will, did
not obsess him as man's did, but he was aware that the
harmony he so admired in Nature depended partly on the
destruction of one form of life by another. This too could
perhaps be amended. A joyous sign of Jupiter's removal, the
Spirit of the Earth said in *Prometheus Unbound*, was when

> Upon a drooping bough with nightshade twined,
> I saw two azure halcyons clinging downward
> And thinning one bright bunch of amber berries
> With quick long beaks.

(III. iv. 79–82)

The kingfishers had become vegetarian, the nightshade had
kept its attractiveness but lost its poison; not by sudden
mystical conversion, but by a gradual extension of human
morality into the realm of sentient Nature that would probably occupy many centuries.

Religion, Philosophy, Morals

Shelley thought all religions both false and true. Their
teachings and institutions were false (though not all equally
so), and had done immense harm. But as allegories, seeking to
explain in terms of the known what was equally unknown to
all men, they embodied some poetic truth.

After a brief adolescent period as 'an enthusiastic Deist',
believing in God as designer of Nature but not as Father or
Saviour, Shelley remained an atheist in the ordinary meaning
of the word. *God*, throughout his poetry, means either 'the

evil deity Christians believe in' (*Letter to the Gisbornes*, l. 25), or something like 'the Power of the universe, whatever it is, which for brevity's sake I am using a conventional and misleading name for' (*Mask of Anarchy*, l. 302). His use of the word is never orthodox. 'I spoke but as ye speak', Demogorgon replies when asked what he means by 'God'. Shelley did not therefore believe Jesus divine, though his admiration for him as a great and daring human reformer and moralist changed very little. His loathing of the Christian religion was also unchanging. Had he enough influence over Byron, he wrote three months before he died, he would certainly 'employ it to eradicate from his great mind the delusions of Christianity'. It was a monstrous superstition; 'no man of sense can think it true'.

One of his most vivid and constant apprehensions, however, was of some Power pervading the universe, the 'overruling Spirit of the collective energy of the moral and material world', non-mental, non-personal, inaccessible, but creative (*plastic*), which pressed up through the living forms of Nature, realized itself imperfectly in works of art, found expression in the doctrines of liberty and equality and in the humane emotions, including sexual love; invested, kindled, sustained, and delighted. This Power, not quite identical with the Universe itself as in Pantheism, was variously called 'Love' or 'the One', and symbolized in imagery of light and fire. Shelley is generally said to be a Platonist, and this is true if taken to mean that he was deeply impressed by Plato as a 'poet', a maker of great metaphors. Plato's famous allegory of the Cave (*The Republic*, VII. 514A–521B) is one of these. Men are imagined chained in an underground prison with their backs to a fire, able to watch only the shadowplay on the wall in front, so accustomed to darkness that the sunlight of the upper world would blind them even if they could reach it. The cave represents our material world; the sunlight is the world of Ideal Forms, of which all earthly things are mere 'shadows'; and a man should spend his life working up from the darkness towards the dazzling reality, from the material to the Eternal. Shelley often used the metaphor, but he was not interested in learning to qualify for another world; for him the Universal Power was something to be co-operated with in its struggle to bring the present world into harmony with itself.

On life after death, Shelley was a hopeful sceptic. Trelawny says that he disbelieved in this, and no personal immortality is contemplated in *Adonais*. The desire to survive after death, he thought, must itself remain the best argument in favour of survival. On all these metaphysical questions he grew less argumentative and more agnostic. 'The soul, or whatever it is'; 'How delightful a picture even if it be not true!' (on Jesus Christ's description of Heaven); 'He wakes or sleeps with the enduring dead.' By mid-1821 he had stopped debating such matters. 'My mind is at peace respecting nothing so much as the constitution and mysteries of the great system of things.'

When writing *Queen Mab* Shelley had been a materialist; but mechanical materialism did not satisfy him, nor did the popular distinction between 'mind' and 'matter'. He seems later to have believed (following Hume and Sir William Drummond) that mind and matter were not opposites but belonged to the same mental unity or continuum, in which individual minds like his own had only a nominally separate existence. But he was always a determinist, believing that all events, mental and otherwise, were controlled by natural law. This belief did not exempt him from the need to choose and act, since men's actions are a vital link in the chain through which Necessity operates (see *Prometheus Unbound*, II. ii. 41–63, pp. 90–91, and note).

Shelley's morals were Benthamite: the object of life was happiness for the greatest number. But true happiness was only attainable through selflessness; and men should live simply, as Rousseau taught—by no means because sensual enjoyment was wrong, but so as to be free for more important enjoyments: social intercourse, art, and science.

Politics

Insight into the class-struggles of contemporary Europe gave Shelley his political starting-point. The age he lived in, that of 'the war of the oppressed against the oppressors', encouraged him to view all development as the result of conflicting opposites: rich and poor, liberty and tyranny, evil and good. He did not really mean to blame the world's misfortunes on 'kings' and 'priests'; these were shorthand expressions for a whole social order and for the delusions that sustained it.

Many radical thinkers, especially Rousseau, Paine, and Godwin, influenced Shelley's wider political theories. For him, all government was ultimately bad; and he condemned arbitrary inequalities of property, including marriage (a 'monopoly of exclusive cohabitation'), together with the power they conferred. A co-operative system must replace all acquisitive systems, or in moral terms (for 'Politics . . . are, in fact, the morals of the nations'), selfishness must become sympathy. 'Affectionate love to and from all', he wrote to Hunt, adding jokingly, 'This ought not only to be the vale of a letter, but a superscription over the gate of life.' First, however, 'the system of society as it exists at present must be overthrown from the foundations with all its superstructure of maxims and forms'. He never thought this would be easy, nor that perfection would follow; like Godwin, he did not believe in perfectibility. Equality 'is unattainable except by a parcel of peas or beans', so is perfection, 'yet . . . the nearer society approaches towards this point the happier will it be.'

These ideals were far removed from the modesty of Shelley's practical short-term proposals for Reform: to disband the army, to abolish tithes and the national debt, to extend but not universalize the franchise. He knew the Reform movement was immature, its organization non-existent; impatience would invite defeat, and worse despotism would follow. 'My principles incite me to take all the good I can get in politics, for ever aspiring to something more,' he told Hunt.

He opposed the use of physical force, because the force of opinion should be sufficient. Yet Shelley, like Godwin, was not an unconditional pacifist: 'So dear is power, that the tyrants themselves neither . . . now, nor ever, left or leave a path to freedom but through their own blood.' What must be avoided at any cost was not force but retaliation, 'the most deadly superstition that ever infested the world'. Revenge for past injury simply perpetuated a sequence of fruitless reprisals; what really mattered was the future.

Poetry and Society

According to Shelley, the greatness of a poet was directly related to the importance of the social movement which called him into existence, and which he in turn helped to make; poets were 'in one sense, the creators, and, in another, the creations of their age. From this subjection the loftiest do not escape'—not even Shakespeare, whom we owed to the humanist awakening that 'shook to dust the oldest and most oppressive form of the Christian religion', while the great contemporary writers were 'companions and forerunners of some unimagined change in our social condition or the opinions which cement it'. When there was no important advance towards a better society, as in Restoration England, there was no important poetry. Consciously or unconsciously, willing and unwilling, poets were 'mirrors of the gigantic shadows which futurity casts upon the present'. But poetry should not try to lay down rules of conduct, or detail a political programme. 'A poem very didactic is I think very stupid.' Poetry 'legislates' by enlarging the imagination so as to show men their own potentialities and heighten their sympathy with their own kind.

SHELLEY'S POETRY

Because one of the two leading periodicals, the Tory *Quarterly Review*, attacked him fiercely while the other, the Whig *Edinburgh Review*, ignored him, Shelley believed at the end of his life that his poetry had failed in spite of his efforts to broaden its appeal. Ollier would not publish *Julian and Maddalo*, a conversational poem; Covent Garden had rejected his play *The Cenci* on moral grounds; even Hunt dared not print *The Mask of Anarchy* or the political songs. Shelley needed an audience, and his apparently total failure to communicate tended to drive his poetry further into ideality and abstraction. 'Nothing is so difficult and unwelcome as to write without a confidence of finding readers.' In fact the lesser critical journals, which Shelley did not see in Italy, gave more space to Shelley's work than to that of other contemporary poets, and it was just the recognition of his powers as a poet that caused their horror of his opinions. Orthodoxy was not indifferent, but afraid. A reviewer fresh from *Queen Mab* felt

as if one of the darkest of the fiends had been clothed with a human body, to enable him to gratify his enmity against the human race, and as if the supernatural atrocity of his hate were only heightened by his power to do injury.

These poems that drew 'oaths from clergymen', and that Shelley himself valued, were the long philosophical ones, *The Revolt of Islam*, *Prometheus Unbound*, *Adonais*; the lyrics were by-products which for the most part he was not sufficiently interested in to publish, or even to complete. After his death the emphasis changed entirely. When Mary Shelley edited his *Posthumous Poems* in 1824, she found and printed over fifty short poems that had not appeared in any of the dozen volumes he had published during his lifetime, and added more in 1839; certain of these, it is now known, she touched-up or rearranged so as to make presentable 'lyrics' out of unfinished fragments. They were a great success. In Palgrave's *Golden Treasury* (1861), the most influential of all English verse anthologies, no fewer than fifteen of the twenty-two short pieces by Shelley had never been published by him, but had been taken from notebooks or from copies given privately to young ladies. By no means all these poems are weak (there are three in the present selection), but when assembled in bulk they seriously overstress a side of Shelley that he did not himself think very important, and they allowed readers to evade the real imaginative challenge of his poetry by concentrating on the sentiment or the fancy.

Some of the best Victorian critics of Shelley, including W. M. Rossetti, Stopford Brooke, and Henry Salt, continued to see the philosophical poems as his central achievement; and Walter Bagehot, who preferred the lyrics, was not tempted by the impulsive qualities he found in them to overlook their other qualities of intellectual control and searching language:

His success . . . is in fragments; and the best of those fragments are lyrical. The very same isolation and suddenness of impulse which rendered him unfit for the composition of great works, rendered him peculiarly fit to pour forth on a sudden the intense essence of peculiar feeling 'in profuse strains of unpremeditated art'. . . . In most poets unearthly beings are introduced to express peculiar removed essences of lyrical rapture; but they are generally failures. . . . In Shelley, such singing solitary beings are almost uniformly success-ful; while writing, his mind really for the moment was in the state in which theirs is supposed always to be. He loved attenuated ideas and abstracted excitement. In expressing their nature he had but to set free his own.

Human nature is not, however, long equal to this sustained effort of remote excitement. . . . It is characteristic of Shelley, that at the end of his most rapturous and sanguine lyrics there intrudes the cold consciousness of this world. . . . In many of his poems the failing of the feeling is as beautiful as its short moment of hope and buoy-ancy. . . .

Nothing in human life to him was inevitable or fixed; he fancied he could alter it all. . . . Where it can, his genius soars from the con-crete and real into the unknown, the indefinite, and the void. . . . We cannot know detail in tracts we have never visited; the infinite has no form; the immeasurable has no outline: that which is common to all worlds is simple. . . . Shelley's excellence in the abstract lyric is almost another phrase for the simplicity of his impulsive imagina-tion. . . .

The abstract idea of beauty is for ever celebrated in Shelley; it haunted his soul. But it was independent of special things; it was the general surface of beauty which lies upon all things. It was the smile of the universe and the expression of the world; it was not the vision of a land of corn and wine. . . .

The peculiarity of his style is its intellectuality; and this strikes us the more from its contrast with his impulsiveness. He had something of this in life. Hurried away by sudden desires as he was in his choice of ends, we are struck with a certain comparative measure and adjust-ment in his choice of means. So in his writings: over the most intense excitement, the grandest objects, the keenest agony, the most buoyant joy, he throws an air of subtle mind. His language is minutely and acutely searching; at the dizziest height of meaning the keenness of the words is greatest.[1]

[1] *The National Review*, October 1856, pp. 369–79.

Most Victorian middle-class readers, however, welcomed the chance to form their image of Shelley from songs that made no great intellectual demands on them, were ideologically harmless, and soared into the infinite, so that his reputation at its highest point—roughly between 1880 and the First World War—depended mainly on such poems as *Oh, world! oh, life! oh, time!*, *To a Skylark*, and *One word is too often profaned*. As late as 1919 A. C. Bradley, a critic of the first rank, was calling Shelley a greater lyrist than Shakespeare.

This view of Shelley the etherial lyrist was strongly reinforced by the legend then current of his seraphic—even semi-divine—character as a man. The legend owed something to Mary Shelley, and a great deal to Hogg, who had his own discreditable reasons for caricaturing the poet in his *Life of Shelley* (1858) as an irresponsible 'eternal child'. The final absurdity was Francis Thompson's immensely popular essay *Shelley*, written in 1889 though not published until 1908: '. . . we peep over the wild mask of revolutionary metaphysics, and we see the winsome face of the child. . . . The universe is his box of toys. He dabbles his fingers in the day-fall. He is gold-dusty with tumbling amidst the stars. He makes bright mischief with the moon. The meteors nuzzle their noses in his hand,' and so on. Common sense was slow to recover ground. When Dowden's great biography came out in 1886, Matthew Arnold's review of it, repeating his earlier description of Shelley as 'a beautiful and ineffectual angel, beating in the void his luminous wings in vain', showed how reluctant readers were to alter their idealized impression of Shelley merely in order to fit the facts. The poet's daughter-in-law, who preserved most of the family papers in a special sanctum near Bournemouth, altered and even burnt documents that contradicted what she wished to believe.

Against this background, the destructiveness of Shelley criticism in the 1920's and 1930's, culminating in F. R. Leavis's *Revaluation* (1936), is seen to be really part of the reaction against Victorian attitudes, not a reassessment of Shelley's best writing, whose edges it barely touched. What the early twentieth century attacked as sentimental, structureless, and cheap were generally the short lyrics so much admired in the previous century, though the attacks even on these were not always more perceptive than the admiration. One Victorian favourite written-off as a self-indulgent display of emotion was *The Indian Serenade* (which Shelley never published):

> O lift me from the grass!
> I die! I faint! I fail!
> Let thy love in kisses rain
> On my cheeks and eyelids pale

But in 1962 a manuscript version turned up entitled *The Indian Girl's Song*, and the lyric proved to be, like several others, not an embarrassing heart-cry from the poet but a dramatic imitation. The main points of the critical attack on Shelley have been summarized best by a critic who did not accept them, Frederick A. Pottle:

He is sentimental: that is, he calls for a greater display of emotion than the modern reader feels to be warranted by the occasion. He employs pronounced, intoxicating, hypnotic rhythms that seem to be trying to sweep the reader into hasty emotional commitments. He seldom uses a firmly held, developed image, but pours out a flood of images which one must grasp momentarily in one aspect and then release. He is fond of figures within figures. He imposes his will on the object of experience: he does not explore 'reality', he flies away from it. He seldom takes a gross, palpable, near-at-hand object from the world of ordinary perception and holds it for contemplation: his gaze goes up to the sky, he starts with objects that are just on the verge of becoming invisible or inaudible or intangible and he strains away even from these. He exhibits dissociation of sensibility: though he is even too much aware of the disgusting, the ugly, the painful, and the horrible, he puts all the beauty into one poem and all the ugliness into another, or he sorts them out in different portions of the same poem. He luxuriates in emotion. He embarrasses the reader by representing himself as weak, frail, bowed, bleeding, fainting, and dying.[1]

Criticism along these lines usefully redefined in modern terms some of the weaknesses that had always been recognized in Shelley's poetry, but its disabling limitation was that its target was the minor Shelley, indeed the bad minor Shelley, of a previous century, not the major poet of *Prometheus Unbound* and *The Triumph of Life*. For parallel with it, a constructive revolution in Shelley studies was beginning in America that has transformed the aspect of his work, although it has not produced fresh criticism so much as rediscovered what there is in the poetry to criticize.

A classic paragraph in A. N. Whitehead's *Science and the Modern World*[2] started one line of inquiry:

Shelley's attitude to science was at the opposite pole to that of Wordsworth. He loved it, and is never tired of expressing in poetry the thoughts which it suggests. It symbolises to him joy, and peace, and illumination. What the hills were to the youth of Wordsworth, a chemical laboratory was to Shelley. It is unfortunate that Shelley's literary critics have, in this respect, so little of Shelley in their own mentality. They tend to treat as a casual oddity of Shelley's nature what was, in fact, part of the main structure of his mind, permeating his poetry through and through. If Shelley had been born a hundred years later, the twentieth century would have seen a Newton among chemists.

[1] *English Romantic Poets: Modern Essays in Criticism*, ed. M. H. Abrams (New York, 1960), p. 297.
[2] (Cambridge, 1926), pp. 122–3.

Twenty years earlier Stopford Brooke had remarked that the lyric *Life of life* was like the dream of a great physicist; but this direct challenge from a distinguished mathematician was taken up by Carl Grabo's *A Newton Among Poets: Shelley's Use of Science in Prometheus Unbound* (1930), which revealed an astonishing wealth of scientific ideas in the poem, and demonstrated that what seems fanciful decoration is often good scientific sense expressed in metaphor. Even when the Fifth Spirit in *Prometheus Unbound* says 'That planet-crested Shape swept by on lightning-braided pinions', the epithets are not pretty poeticalities: the Shape carries the emblem of Venus and is moving on 'wings interwoven with electricity'; that is, the energy of Love is expressed as electrical energy. Electricity or 'lightning', subtle, potent, all-pervading, is the counterpart in the physical world of Love in the moral world. So 'love' can be a metaphor for electricity (*The Cloud*, ll. 22–28), and 'electricity' a metaphor for sexual or spiritual love (*The Triumph of Life*, ll. 155–60). Like Shelley's other symbols, lightning may also assume an opposite, evil function, as in the form of Jupiter's thunderbolts; love's energies can be perverted to hatred.

Grabo made Shelley's readers fully aware for the first time of how constantly but unobtrusively concepts such as electrical energy, the atomic structure of matter, the organization of outer space, evolution, infra-red radiation, are used in the poetry, so that the most apparently vaporous imagery may have its nucleus of hard fact at the centre. A professional scientist, Desmond King-Hele, who has confirmed the main findings of this pioneer work, suggested in trying to define Shelley's scientific attitude of mind in his poetry that probably

its most important component is persistent analysis of Nature: being eager to delve beneath the surface of appearance, instead of seeing things whole like Keats and Shakespeare; searching out the causal chain between one facet of Nature and another, and linking those facets imaginatively or metaphorically to interpret the scene described. . . . Shelley often cheats Time, at some cost in obscurity, by avoiding jargon and using scientific theory as the basis for an imaginative jump. Though the theory may have proved in part erroneous, its modern version often enables us to see the logic of the jump; we take a different path to the same endpoint.[1]

Thanks to Grabo and others Shelley has come to be recognized as in many respects a very exact poet, one who paid the workings of the physical universe inquisitive and continuous attention, observing the world he lived in as closely as he followed the progress of scientific speculation about it. In the lines quoted on page 21 from *Prometheus Unbound*, what the kingfishers are pictured as eating is not deadly nightshade, whose berries are black, but *solanum dulcamara*, bittersweet, which has fruit of different colours on the same bunch; the birds are 'thinning' the unripe orange berries by eating the redder ripe ones. The observed fact or the scientific theory is not, in most cases, the thing directly contemplated, but provides an analogy for a moral 'idealism' or the basis for a poetic myth; here the physical details are incidental to the moral change they illustrate, but they are, as usual, recorded with precision. The point is important because critics who disparaged Shelley's mind for its inability to hold an object steadily in front of it were sometimes so unfamiliar with their own natural environment that they could not recognize what object Shelley's mind was holding.

A second line of investigation, not entirely separable from the first, started from Yeats's belief expressed in *Ideas of Good and Evil* (1903) that many of Shelley's images had the definiteness

[1] *Shelley: His Thought and Work* (London, 1960), p. 166.

and the systematic recurrence of symbols. This suggestion, too, was followed up by Carl Grabo in *The Magic
Plant: The Growth of Shelley's Thought* (1936), and by other
books which explored Shelley's symbolic language. Why,
Grabo asked,

if Shelley so loved clarity, are some of his greater poems difficult?
There are two forms of obscurity. One is born of simple muddle-
headedness; the other is born of difficult and subtle ideas, or of an
unfamiliar language. Shelley is difficult partly because he had a subtle
mind which played with fine distinctions of thought, but more
because he came gradually to the employment of a language with
which most modern readers are wholly unfamiliar. He developed a
symbolic form of expression which must be studied to be understood;
its derivation must be traced.[1]

Grabo, like Yeats before him, traced this symbolism mainly
to the Neo-Platonists. Neo-Platonism, a system of doctrine
based on mystical interpretations of Plato's writings, had been
expounded to English readers in the commentaries of Thomas
Taylor, some of whose translations Shelley used. According
to this system, for example, the water-cycle which appears so
often in Shelley's poetry, wherein water drawn up by the
sun from the sea is carried inland in rainclouds, precipitated
as rain or dew, and returns to the sea by way of springs and
rivers, symbolizes the transit of human souls through earthly
existence. Souls drawn from the sea of Universal Being are
born into the realm of matter or 'descend into generation', as
rain falls from the clouds, and travel down the stream of life
(perhaps in boats) to rejoin the sea and await rebirth. Clouds,
and the various forms of water, are therefore symbols of
material or spiritual fertility. A fountain (i.e. a spring) can
mean intellectual illumination, and the cave where it rises

[1] Carl Grabo, *The Meaning of 'The Witch of Atlas'* (Chapel Hill, North
Carolina, 1935), p. vi.

may stand for the mind, or for material life shut away from the spiritual world.

Such ideas may help to interpret Shelley's meaning, though they do not necessarily derive from Neo-Platonism, and others among Shelley's recurrent symbols owe a great deal directly to Plato: for instance, the *shadow* or reflected image, which may derive from Plato's theory that all earthly forms are merely 'shadows' of their prototypes in the Ideal World, or from the allegory of the Cave (see pp. 22–23); and the *veil*, a material barrier concealing the true, the beautiful, or the infinite. But many symbols such as the *storm* and the *volcano* are neither Platonic nor Neo-Platonic; and Peter Butter, while agreeing that Shelley used a symbolic language, concluded that it would be wrong to translate it in any mechanical or systematic way:

The recurrence of some of these words is too frequent to be accidental; and Shelley's landscapes are often too fantastic and too carefully elaborated to be mere pieces of natural description. The precise significance of any image varies with its context, and no explanation can ever exhaust its possible meanings. A poetic image is never a mere counter—worth so much and no more and always the same amount. Indeed the author himself may not be able to say exactly why his mind returns so often to certain favourite ideas. . . .

One could make a graduated scale of images in accordance with the extent to which they are symbolic. At one extreme would be the purely descriptive, by which a picture is conveyed to the mind without any underlying significance. . . . At the other end would be images which are purely symbolic, purely intellectual. Examples of these in Shelley are the eagle and the snake at the beginning of *The Revolt of Islam*. These symbols have not grown out of his experience, but have been consciously thought of. . . . Between these two extremes are all those images in which there is, in varying degrees, some fusion of sense, feeling and thought, or at least two of these. . . . Of course it is not desirable that all levels of significance should be perfectly definite and explicable; poetry of that kind is arid. What one wants, and gets in the best of Shelley, is a hard core with an aura of suggestion round it.[1]

Butter's example of a 'purely intellectual' image, an eagle and a snake locked in combat, represents the conflict of tyranny with freedom, evil with good, in Canto I of *The Revolt of Islam* and in the poetry generally. Why those particular creatures, and why that way round? The eagle, a bird of prey, was Jupiter's cruel and obscene pet (*P.U.*, I. 34), an emblem of Imperial Rome, of Napoleon, and of arbitrary royal power. The snake symbolizes liberty and good because Shelley, like most men familiar with wild life in boyhood, thought it a beautiful creature (*Mask of Anarchy*, l. 111); because it is an ancient symbol of fertility and rebirth, associated with the sun (*Adonais*, ll. 161–2; *Hellas*, Chorus II, ll. 3–4); because it is lowly, oppressed, and maligned, yet can bite (*Mask of Anarchy*, l. 233); and because Satan had been turned into a snake by the tyrannous God against whom he had rebelled. This last Satanic association links the *snake* with *Lucifer*, the Morning Star ('How art thou fallen from heaven, o Lucifer, son of the morning!'—Isaiah xiv. 12); and as the Morning Star is really Venus, the planet of Love, the *snake*, tyranny's victim, can be identified with *Love*, tyranny's destined conqueror. Both eagle and snake may also appear in their ordinary, popular significations: one as a king of birds (*Laon and Cythna*, IX. xxv. 9) and a sun-lover (*Triumph of Life*, l. 131), the other as a poisonous reptile (*Adonais*, l. 317). The context must decide which of the symbolic associations, if any, are relevant in each case.

An 'aura of suggestion', on the other hand, does not necessarily entail vagueness, as the word *intoxication* illustrates. Shelley drank little alcohol and hated drunkenness, which

[1] *Shelley's Idols of the Cave* (Edinburgh, 1954), pp. 59, 216–17.

deprived men of reason, so it was natural for the ruling-class hooligans in *The Mask of Anarchy*, like their originals at Peterloo, to be

> Drunk as with intoxication
> Of the wine of desolation.

But it was possible to be intoxicated, even deprived of reason, in a way that was good. This could happen when Necessity, or the force of the Ideal manifested through Nature, so possessed a man that its impulse transcended rational thought and drove him to great action, or prophecy, or art. When immediately after the semichorus on pages 90–91, Asia and Panthea reach the volcanic mountain of Demogorgon, they see rising from its crater a vapour

> Which lonely men drink wandering in their youth
> And call truth, virtue, love, genius, or joy,
> That maddening wine of life, whose dregs they drain
> To deep intoxication, and uplift
> Like Maenads who cry loud, Evoe! Evoe!
> The voice which is contagion to the world.
> > (*Prometheus Unbound*, II. iii. 5–10)

That is, young thinkers and poets, excited by ideals absorbed from the age they live in, are inspired to propagate them. Maenads, followers of Bacchus, could thus represent either 'disorganization' or 'reproduction'; from one aspect their drunken frenzy round the god of wine was a superstition, an insult to reason; from another aspect their total possession by the great fertility-god resembled the inspiration of the poet by the Universal Power's life-renewing energy (see Appendix B). Both aspects might combine in one image; for example, the Maenad's 'bright hair' in the *Ode to the West Wind* suggests the fertilizing power of the storm as well as its destructive wildness. All these words, therefore, *intoxication, wine,*

Maenads, maddening, contagion, may require to be taken at more than their face-value in Shelley's poetry, and each is reversible—that is, may have an opposite implication in another context. The *wine of life* is the antithesis of the *wine of desolation*; *contagion,* implying the enthusiastic spread of enlightenment in the passage above, describes a contaminating stain in *Adonais* (l. 356). These associations are not private or arbitrary, but are already in the words; only we must learn Shelley's emphases and allow particular contexts to release the right ones.

Through the growing understanding of Shelley's symbolic language it has been realized that however deceptively fluent and 'beautiful' Shelley's verse may appear on the surface, it is hardly ever quite as simple as it looks, and always needs to be read with the intelligence switched fully on. One reason why it is so easy to read Shelley lazily is that the vogue of his own poetry, superficially-understood, has worked against him: a vast quantity of lazy stuff in Shelley's manner, though without his intellectual content, has been written between his day and ours. Moreover, as John Holloway has reminded us, all the Romantic poets read uncomfortably at times because of expressions that have since been debased in meaning or emotional tone but not sufficiently long ago for historical allowances to be made. Thus it is easier to accept the quaintness of 'Jonson's learnèd sock' in *L'Allegro* than to remember, when limbs are described in one of Shelley's most impassioned lyrics as burning 'Through the vest which seems to hide them', that the modern undergarment only came in with Queen Victoria. Shelley, it is agreed by all, had little sensuous feeling for words as things-in-themselves, materials of art; he used words as signs for things, or for concepts. His temptation, when not writing at full pressure, was to use words picked from habit out of a compulsively narrow stock, when their ordinary meanings were insufficiently specific and when their symbolic overtones were irrelevant. Then the continual stars, dews, winds, and mists, any of which may be bright, faint, pale, keen, or dim, become pointless and wearisome. No idiom can escape the weakness of its characteristic strength.

The recognition of Shelley's essential sanity as a social and political thinker was a third major critical advance of the mid-twentieth century. Newman Ivey White's new standard biography *Shelley* (1940) made this recognition inevitable by its firm correction of the 'eternal child' legend and its objective treatment of his ideas as intelligent and responsible. Among working-class readers Shelley's political ideas had been taken seriously ever since the first pirated copy of *Queen Mab* appeared in 1821, but middle-class readers either hushed them up or else, as in H. N. Brailsford's clever but misleading study of 1913,[1] blamed them all on Godwin. Bernard Shaw had already pointed out that

Shelley was not a hot-headed nor an unpractical person. All his writings, whether in prose or verse, have a peculiarly deliberate quality. His political pamphlets are unique in their freedom from all appeal to the destructive passions; there is neither anger, sarcasm, nor frivolity in them; and in this respect his poems exactly resemble his political pamphlets.[2]

Shaw had not read Shelley's ninety-page essay *A Philosophical View of Reform* (1819), unpublished until 1920 and never yet made generally accessible to English readers, but his view was fully borne out by its cool, methodical tracing of the struggle for political liberty in Europe up to the year of Peterloo, and its level-headed programme for the future. On the basis of this new material, Kenneth Neill Cameron made detailed studies during the 1940's and 1950's of Shelley's social and

[1] *Shelley, Godwin and Their Circle* (London, 2nd ed. 1951).
[2] *Pen Portraits and Reviews by Bernard Shaw* (London, 1932), p. 240.

political thought in relation to his poetry, showing it to be reasoned, temperate, and coherent; not over-dependent on Godwin, although consciously belonging to a European Radical tradition. However wrong Shelley's views may have been, Cameron has made it impossible to dismiss them as childish or absurd. And just as the imagery often depends on a hard core of science, so the idealistic visions of the poems are now seen to rest on this basis of firmly reasoned prose.

The final outcome of these various studies has been, in effect, to reverse the Victorian order of priority and re-focus attention on the long poems, with increased respect for their intellectual content and poetic structure. The gradually-improving understanding of what is really in the poems, and how they work, has led to a distinct shift of taste: a tendency to depreciate what is unrelatedly personal and emotional in Shelley's poetry, and to look for its real strength in the familiar, the thoughtful, the ironical, the urbane. Some readers will think this emphasis wrong, but it corresponds much more closely to Shelley's own than the one it has superseded. Probably few critics would now agree that Shelley was essentially a lyric poet, at least without adding that he was a lyric poet of a very peculiar kind. The variety of his best work is surprisingly wide—wider than that of any other English Romantic poet. The present short selection contains lyrical drama (*Prometheus*, *Hellas*); political balladry (*The Mask of Anarchy*); lyrics serious (*Lines*), playful (*Love's Philosophy*), and mythopoeic (*The Cloud*); the familiar epistle (*Letter to the Gisbornes*); elegy (*Adonais*); and narrative (*Laon and Cythna*). A complete list of 'kinds' would have to include straight tragedy (*The Cenci*); burlesque (*Swellfoot*); comic satire (*Peter Bell the Third*), and epigram. This variety must be set against the reputed narrowness of Shelley's range.

A shrewd critic himself, Shelley had a good idea of what

was original and unique in his own poetry, and was also the first to record those objections to it that have been repeated in various forms of words ever since. 'My friends say my *Prometheus* is too wild, ideal, and perplexed with imagery. It may be so.' Before this he had admitted to Godwin that he was conscious in what he wrote 'of an absence of that tranquillity which is the attribute and accompaniment of power'. But his best-known self-criticism, the wry comment to the Gisbornes on *Epipsychidion*, was typically double-edged:

As to real flesh & blood, you know that I do not deal in those articles; you might as well go to a ginshop for a leg of mutton, as expect any thing human or earthly from me.

Self-mocking as this may be, it is also a challenge to current taste. Shelley was a vegetarian, and disapproved of mutton almost as much as he did of gin; he is implying that genuine poetry will avoid both crude naturalism and artificial stimulants—the two literary demands, he thought, of the new wealthy middle classes, who wanted 'either the antitype [=replica] of their own mediocrity in books, or such stupid and distorted and inharmonious idealisms as alone have the power to stir their torpid imaginations'. His own 'idealisms' (imaginative visions) aspired to neither condition. Bees in the ivy-bloom (p. 85) were not in themselves a poet's proper subject but a mere starting-point for poetry: still, they are accurately observed, and what is finally to be created from them are 'forms more real than living man'—not a photograph or an alcoholic dream but an intensification of reality.

Some of the difficulties entailed for the reader by this intensification have been discussed by John Holloway:

. . . Shelley is hard to read not only because his language and indeed his punctuation are not quite our own, not only because what he intends to convey is sometimes condensed and esoteric, not only because his intelligence is dexterous enough, and in evidence enough, often to make what he writes more intricate than the work of others. It is difficult because there is, with trying regularity, a tension and an eagerness about it that leads the reader hardly to expect the control which he very often finds. One might almost put this point by saying that Shelley's sensibility was too emphatically unified to be altogether tolerable. No one ought to feel so passionately, so intensely as this, and yet move in thought with such virtuosity. Or perhaps it is better put as an excessive demand which Shelley makes on his readers; but it is not an excess merely in the sense of being above the powers of ordinary able men, it is an excess in which there is a hint of eccentricity, or rather of hypertrophy. If these powers are to be as great as these, others must suffer—a price is to be paid. Often enough in Shelley, and on a final judgment, I think, over his work seen as a whole, the price is a fatiguing intensity of intellectual and emotional response, within a range which is fatiguing in its narrowness. Only in *The Triumph of Life*, at the very end of his career, does one hear, sustained throughout a long and wholly serious work, that note of composure and calm, and indeed of dry shrewdness, which offers the reader of this very difficult poem a kind of reassurance new in Shelley.[1]

There is certainly a discrepancy, at times a contradiction, between the swift onrush of the language and the complexity of the thought, or density of the symbolic meaning, which the language embodies or glances at. The movement of the verse, and its shifting, impalpable subject-matter, urges fast reading and light reactions; the complex meaning requires slow, unrelaxed concentration. Shelley's mind seems to have worked faster, intellectually and emotionally at once, than the minds of any of his readers, and because he lacked an audience he never learned to allow for the difference.

The restlessness of Shelley's verse can also be very tiring,

[1] *Selected Poems of Percy Bysshe Shelley* (London, 1960), p. xxxiii.

but it reflects a particular and unique apprehension of reality. David Perkins has described

the constant motion that Shelley notices in the natural world; he seldom presents anything that suggests repose or permanence. Even those objects that another poet might have used as metaphors of rest and stillness are observed to be darting or dancing. One thinks of Keats's sonnet which employs a 'Bright Star' as a symbol precisely because it appears to be 'stedfast'. In Shelley's poetry even the stars 'whirl and flee,/Like a swarm of golden bees'. A star 'scatters drops of golden light' until 'it is borne away, away/By the swift Heavens that cannot stay'; the earth, instead of following its slow planetary orbit, 'dances about the sun'. Similarly, if he pictures a mountain, he may see not the Wordsworthian stillness, but a 'sun-awakened avalanche'. In fact, images of repose and solidity in Shelley's poetry seem to exist mainly to dramatize the force that shakes them.[1]

The contrast noticed by many other critics, notably Richard Harter Fogle,[2] between Keats's descriptive language of solidity and achieved repose, *steadfast, embalmèd, gluts,* and Shelley's of process and struggle, *swift, eagle-baffling, unbuild,* points to something much more fundamental than a difference of style: Shelley's attitude to change. Most lyric poetry is a cry of anguish against transience: loss; altered love; beauty that passes; physical death. Yet life has evolved through biological change, and persists from moment to moment by changing. Shelley is distinctive in that although he imagined and desired 'Elysian, windless, fortunate abodes' of social and sexual equality, where Nature would be wholly under man's co-operative control—where, in Platonic metaphor, the Many would be identical with the One—he accepted imaginatively the processes of change that alone could lead towards

[1] *The Quest for Permanence* (Harvard, 1959), p. 117.
[2] *The Imagery of Keats and Shelley* (Chapel Hill, North Carolina, 1949).

such a goal. The goal itself he knew to be unattainable, because his very acceptance of change gave him also a quite exceptional awareness of man's situation in infinite time, of the limited and relative nature of every human society and attribute. All other poets reject change emotionally even when their reason acknowledges it to be inevitable. Shelley's uniqueness is that in some of his best poetry his whole poetic personality sides with change, with the shadow of the sunrise, with the uncontrollable Wind, with Time that has shattered Ozymandias, with Demogorgon who will overthrow Jupiter. 'And yet to me welcome is day and night', Prometheus cries, embracing the suffering that temporal existence inflicts on him. In the Platonic metaphors he often uses, Shelley does not normally look forward to escaping from the flux of reality into some transcendental permanent world, but seeks unity with the Ideal in its incessant struggle to realize itself through the transient things of Nature and of human society,

> bursting in its beauty and its might
> From trees and beasts and men into the Heavens' light.

To the individual man, however, the pain of transience is not diminished by taking the side of change; instead the co-existence of the two feelings contributes to that peculiar poignancy that is characteristic of Shelley's utterance. In his best writing, personal suffering is felt as a qualifying force that accompanies, without counteracting, the main affirmative movement of the poem. 'What if my leaves are falling like its own?' Shelley is almost invariably strongest in poems where the social, the natural, and the personal worlds coincide, weakest when he is most purely personal.

Whether poetry with these characteristics merely blurs what is distinct in actuality, or whether it can give a unique and moving insight into men and Nature, will go on being argued. Conflict seems to be inherent in Shelley's poetry, as it was in his view of the world and in the actions of his life. Perhaps for this very reason Shelley is the only great English poet outside the twentieth century who would be entirely at home—though not, it may be, much happier than he was—among the social changes, scientific triumphs, and political struggles of today.

SHELLEY'S LIFE

1792 Born at Field Place, near Horsham, Sussex (4 August), son of Timothy Shelley, landowner and Whig M.P.

1804–10 At Eton.

Zastrozzi, 'Gothic' novel, published (1810).

1811 Expelled (with Hogg) in his second term at University College, Oxford, for *The Necessity of Atheism* (March).

Elopes with Harriet Westbrook, married in Edinburgh (August).

1812 Agitating in Ireland for political emancipation (February–March).

Meets Godwin in London (October).

1813 *Queen Mab* published (May).

Ianthe born (June).

1814 War ended in Europe (April).

Elopes with Mary Godwin (July); tours Continent, together with Claire Clairmont.

Charles born to Harriet (November).

Struggle against debts and ill-health.

1815 Through death of grandfather, begins to receive annual income of £800 (June).

Battle of Waterloo (18 June).

1816 William born (January).

Alastor published (February).

Second Continental tour; with Byron on Lake of Geneva (summer).

Economic distress and rioting in England.

Harriet's suicide; marries Mary Godwin (December).

Friendship with Leigh Hunt.

1817 Allegra, Claire's daughter by Byron, born (January).

Now meeting Keats (February).

Deprived by Lord Eldon's judgement of Harriet's two children (March).

1817 Living at Marlow on the Thames, in touch with Peacock,
Hogg, the Hunts (from March).

Clara born (September).

In ill-health (autumn).

Laon and Cythna printed (December).

1818 *The Revolt of Islam* published, modified from *Laon and Cythna*
(January).

Leaves for Italy (March).

Meets the Gisbornes (May).

Translates Plato's *Symposium* (July).

Visits Byron and Allegra in Venice (August; scene of *Julian
and Maddalo*).

Clara dies, aged 1 (September).

Writing *Prometheus Unbound*, Act I (autumn).

Visits Naples, Vesuvius, Bay of Baiae (December).

1819 Finishes *Prometheus Unbound*, Acts II and III, in Rome (March–
April).

Finishes *Julian and Maddalo* (May).

William dies, aged $3\frac{1}{2}$ (June); moves to Leghorn.

Writing *The Cenci* (summer).

Distress, agitation, and repression in England.

Peterloo (16 August).

Writes *The Mask of Anarchy* (September).

Moves to Florence; writes *Peter Bell the Third*, *Ode to the West
Wind* (October).

Writing *Prometheus Unbound*, Act IV (autumn), and *A Philosophical View of Reform* (October–December).

Percy Florence born (12 November).

Meets Sophia Stacey (November).

Writes *England in 1819* (December).

1820 Moves to Pisa (January).

The Cenci published (spring).

News of Spanish revolution (March).

Writes *Ode to Liberty*, *To a Skylark* (June), and *Letter to the
Gisbornes* (July).

Constitution proclaimed in Naples (July).

1820 *The Witch of Atlas, Ode to Naples* written, and *Prometheus Unbound* published (August).

Writes *Swellfoot the Tyrant* (August–September).

Friendship with Emilia Viviani (from December).

1821 Edward and Jane Williams arrive (January).

The Naples revolution crushed (February).

Writes *A Defence of Poetry* (February–March).

First news of the Greek rising (1 April).

News of Keats's death in Rome on 23 February arrives (mid-April).

Death of Napoleon (5 May).

Adonais written (May–June), printed in Pisa (July).

Epipsychidion published anonymously (summer).

Hellas written (October).

1822 Trelawny arrives (January).

Writes *The Invitation, The Recollection, To Jane: With a Guitar; Hellas* published (spring).

Allegra dies in a convent (19 April).

Moves, with the Williamses, to Casa Magni on the Bay of Spezzia (April).

The *Don Juan* arrives (12 May).

Writing *The Triumph of Life* (May–June).

Lines written in the Bay of Lerici (June).

Drowned with Williams while sailing back from welcoming the Hunts to Italy (8 July).

1823 Shelley's ashes interred in Protestant Cemetery, Rome.

1824 *Posthumous Poems of Percy Bysshe Shelley* published by Mary Shelley.

SELECT BIBLIOGRAPHY

I. EDITIONS OF SHELLEY'S WORKS

(a) *Collected Works*

    Complete Poetical Works, ed. T. Hutchinson. Oxford Standard Authors edition (Oxford, 1904).

(b) *Selections*

    Selected Poems of Percy Bysshe Shelley, ed. John Holloway (London, 1960).

    Peacock's Four Ages of Poetry. Shelley's Defence of Poetry. Browning's Essay on Shelley, ed. H. F. B. Brett-Smith (Oxford, 1921).

    'Shelley's Translations from Plato: a Critical Edition.' Included in James A. Notopoulos, *The Platonism of Shelley* (Durham, N.C., 1949).

II. BIOGRAPHY AND CRITICISM

(a) *Books*

    Edmund Blunden, *Shelley. A Life Story* (London, 1946). The best short life.

    Newman Ivey White, *Shelley*. 2 vols. (London, 1947). The standard life (first published in America in 1940) with accounts of many poems.

    Carlos Baker, *Shelley's Major Poetry: The Fabric of a Vision* (Princeton, 1948). Suggests interpretations of the longer poems only.

    Kenneth Neill Cameron, *The Young Shelley: Genesis of a Radical* (New York, 1950; London, 1951). A thorough study of Shelley's career and ideas, up to the end of 1814 only.

    P. H. Butter, *Shelley's Idols of the Cave* (Edinburgh, 1954). Explores the images and symbolism, scientific and Platonic.

    Desmond King-Hele, *Shelley, His Thought and Work* (London, 1960). A sympathetic all-round introduction by a professional scientist.

(b) *Articles*

    Bernard Shaw, 'Shaming the Devil about Shelley' (1892), reprinted in *Pen Portraits and Reviews* (London, 1932). A good corrective to the 'ineffectual angel' tradition in criticism.

    English Romantic Poets: Modern Essays in Criticism, ed. M. H. Abrams (New York, 1960). Reprints four influential essays:

    F. R. Leavis, 'Shelley' (1936).

    C. S. Lewis, 'Shelley, Dryden, and Mr. Eliot' (1939).

    Frederick A. Pottle, 'The Case of Shelley' (1952, revised).

    Donald Davie, 'Shelley's Urbanity' (1953).

NOTE ON THE TEXT

Almost all Shelley's poems, even those printed in his life-time, were copied out or seen through the press by others, so that most of them have complicated textual histories. Only an indication, therefore, of the basic texts is given below. All the relevant editions and manuscripts known to the editor have been consulted for this new version of the poems. The aim with each poem has been to reproduce, as faithfully as clarity allows, the arrangement that seems to have satisfied its author. Many silent changes have been made, especially in punctuation, to reproduce as closely as possible Shelley's autograph practice.

Mutability is reprinted from *Alastor* (1816); *Stanzas*, from *Laon and Cythna* (1818); and *Ozymandias* from *Rosalind and Helen* (1819). The text of *Prometheus Unbound* is based on the first collected edition of 1839, revised from Shelley's holo-graphs in the Bodleian Library.[1] *The Mask of Anarchy* is from Shelley's holograph (Wise MS., British Museum), supple-mented by Mary Shelley's corrected transcript (Hunt MS., Library of Congress). The *Ode to the West Wind* is from *Prometheus Unbound* (1820). *Love's Philosophy, England in 1819*, and *Song*, are from Shelley's holographs at Eton College, in the Bodleian Library, and at Harvard respectively. *An Exhortation, To a Skylark*, and *The Cloud* (corrected from the 1839 edition and from the Bodleian holographs), are from *Prometheus Unbound* (1820). The text of *Letter to the Gisbornes* (retitled) is that of John Gisborne's annotated copy of *Post-humous Poems* (1824), supplemented by Mary Shelley's trans-script (Huntington Library) and by the original draft

[1] This work was greatly helped by *Shelley's Prometheus Unbound: A Variorum Edition*, ed. L. J. Zillman (Seattle, 1959).

(Bodleian Library). *The Pursued and the Pursuer* is reprinted from *Stand*, vol. V, no. 3 (1961). *Apollo Sings* (retitled from Mary Shelley's *Midas*) is from Shelley's holograph in the Bodleian Library. *Adonais*, reprinted from the first edition, 1821, incorporates corrections Mary Shelley made in the collected edition of 1839 checked against Shelley's drafts in the Bodleian Library. *The Aziola* is based on the earliest of Mary Shelley's transcripts (Bodleian Library). The *Hellas* choruses are reprinted from the first edition, 1822, with punctuation slightly revised from the Williams' transcript (Huntington Library). *To Jane. The Invitation* is from Shelley's holograph in the Cambridge University Library, corrected from Mary Shelley's transcript of the lost draft (Bodleian Library). *The Triumph of Life* and *Lines* are reprinted from *Studia Neophilologica*, vol. xxxii, no. 2 (1960), and *The Review of English Studies*, vol. xii, no. 45 (February 1961) respectively (both from holograph drafts in the Bodleian Library).

The text of *The Defence of Poetry* is that of the first edition, *Essays, Letters from Abroad, Translations and Fragments*, ed. Mrs. Shelley (1840), with four corrections from A. H. Koszul, *Shelley's Prose in the Bodleian Manuscripts* (London, 1910).

Appendix B is printed, by permission, from James A. Notopoulos's edition of Shelley's translations from Plato, in *The Platonism of Shelley* (Durham, N.C., 1949).

Mutability

Alastor (1816)

WE are as clouds that veil the midnight moon;
  How restlessly they speed, and gleam, and quiver,
Streaking the darkness radiantly!—yet soon
  Night closes round, and they are lost for ever:

Or like forgotten lyres, whose dissonant strings   5
  Give various response to each varying blast,
To whose frail frame no second motion brings
  One mood or modulation like the last.

We rest.—A dream has power to poison sleep;
  We rise.—One wandering thought pollutes the day;   10
We feel, conceive or reason, laugh or weep;
  Embrace fond woe, or cast our cares away:

It is the same!—For, be it joy or sorrow,
  The path of its departure still is free:
Man's yesterday may ne'er be like his morrow;   15
  Nought may endure but Mutability.

Stanzas from Laon and Cythna
Written summer 1817. Published 1818

'THE blasts of autumn drive the wingèd seeds
  Over the earth,—next come the snows, and rain,
  And frosts, and storms, which dreary winter leads
  Out of his Scythian cave, a savage train;
  Behold! Spring sweeps over the world again,   5
  Shedding soft dews from her etherial wings;
  Flowers on the mountains, fruits over the plain,
  And music on the waves and woods she flings,
And love on all that lives, and calm on lifeless things.

'O Spring, of hope, and love, and youth, and gladness 10
  Wind-wingèd emblem! brightest, best and fairest!
  Whence comest thou, when, with dark winter's sadness
  The tears that fade in sunny smiles thou sharest?
  Sister of joy, thou art the child who wearest
  Thy mother's dying smile, tender and sweet;   15
  Thy mother Autumn, for whose grave thou bearest
  Fresh flowers, and beams like flowers, with gentle feet,
Disturbing not the leaves which are her winding-sheet.

'Virtue, and Hope, and Love, like light and Heaven,
  Surround the world.—We are their chosen slaves.   20
  Has not the whirlwind of our spirit driven
  Truth's deathless germs to thought's remotest caves?
  Lo, Winter comes!—the grief of many graves,
  The frost of death, the tempest of the sword,
  The flood of tyranny, whose sanguine waves   25
  Stagnate like ice at Faith the enchanter's word,
And bind all human hearts in its repose abhorred.

'The seeds are sleeping in the soil: meanwhile
The tyrant peoples dungeons with his prey,
Pale victims on the guarded scaffold smile   30
Because they cannot speak; and, day by day,
The moon of wasting Science wanes away
Among her stars, and in that darkness vast
The Sons of Earth to their foul Idols pray,
And grey priests triumph, and like blight or blast   35
A shade of selfish care o'er human looks is cast.

'This is the winter of the world;—and here
We die, even as the winds of Autumn fade,
Expiring in the frore and foggy air.—
Behold! Spring comes, though we must pass, who made   40
The promise of its birth, even as the shade
Which from our death, as from a mountain, flings
The future, a broad sunrise; thus arrayed
As with the plumes of overshadowing wings,
From its dark gulf of chains, Earth like an eagle springs.'   45

Ozymandias

Published January 1818

I MET a traveller from an antique land
Who said: Two vast and trunkless legs of stone
Stand in the desert. Near them, on the sand,
Half sunk, a shattered visage lies, whose frown,
And wrinkled lip, and sneer of cold command,   5
Tell that its sculptor well those passions read
Which yet survive, stamped on these lifeless things,
The hand that mocked them and the heart that fed:

And on the pedestal these words appear:
'My name is Ozymandias, king of kings: 10
Look on my works, ye Mighty, and despair!'
Nothing beside remains. Round the decay
Of that colossal wreck, boundless and bare
The lone and level sands stretch far away.

Prometheus Unbound

Act I

Written autumn 1818. *Prometheus Unbound* (1820)

SCENE, a ravine of icy rocks in the Indian Caucasus.
PROMETHEUS is discovered bound to the precipice. PANTHEA
and IONE are seated at his feet. Time, night. During the
scene, morning slowly breaks.

Prometheus. Monarch of Gods and Daemons, and all Spirits
   But One, who throng those bright and rolling worlds
   Which Thou and I alone of living things
   Behold with sleepless eyes! regard this Earth
   Made multitudinous with thy slaves, whom thou   5
   Requitest for knee-worship, prayer and praise,
   And toil, and hecatombs of broken hearts,
   With fear and self-contempt and barren hope;
   Whilst me, who am thy foe, eyeless in hate,
   Hast thou made reign and triumph, to thy scorn,   10
   O'er mine own misery and thy vain revenge.
   Three thousand years of sleep-unsheltered hours,
   And moments aye divided by keen pangs
   Till they seem years, torture and solitude,
   Scorn and despair,—these are mine empire.   15

More glorious far than that which thou surveyest
From thine unenvied throne, O Mighty God!
Almighty, had I deigned to share the shame
Of thine ill tyranny, and hung not here
Nailed to this wall of eagle-baffling mountain,   20
Black, wintry, dead, unmeasured; without herb,
Insect, or beast, or shape or sound of life—
Ah me, alas, pain, pain ever, forever!

No change, no pause, no hope! Yet I endure.
I ask the Earth, have not the mountains felt?   25
I ask yon Heaven—the all-beholding Sun,
Has it not seen? the Sea, in storm or calm
Heaven's ever-changing Shadow, spread below,
Have its deaf waves not heard my agony?
Ah me, alas, pain, pain ever, forever!   30

The crawling glaciers pierce me with the spears
Of their moon-freezing crystals; the bright chains
Eat with their burning cold into my bones.
Heaven's wingèd hound, polluting from thy lips
His beak in poison not its own, tears up   35
My heart; and shapeless sights come wandering by,
The ghastly people of the realm of dream,
Mocking me: and the Earthquake-fiends are charged
To wrench the rivets from my quivering wounds
When the rocks split and close again behind;   40
While from their loud abysses howling throng
The genii of the storm, urging the rage
Of whirlwind, and afflict me with keen hail.
And yet to me welcome is day and night,
Whether one breaks the hoar frost of the morn,   45
Or starry, dim, and slow, the other climbs

The leaden-coloured east; for then they lead
Their wingless, crawling Hours, one among whom
—As some dark Priest hales the reluctant victim—
Shall drag thee, cruel King, to kiss the blood   50
From these pale feet, which then might trample thee
If they disdained not such a prostrate slave.
Disdain? ah no, I pity thee. What ruin
Will hunt thee undefended through wide Heaven!
How will thy soul, cloven to its depth with terror,   55
Gape like a Hell within! I speak in grief
Not exultation, for I hate no more
As then, ere misery made me wise. The Curse
Once breathed on thee I would recall. Ye Mountains,
Whose many-voicèd Echoes, through the mist   60
Of cataracts, flung the thunder of that spell;
Ye icy Springs, stagnant with wrinkling frost,
Which vibrated to hear me, and then crept
Shuddering through India; thou serenest Air,
Through which the Sun walks burning without beams, 65
And ye swift Whirlwinds, who on poisèd wings
Hung mute and moveless o'er yon hushed abyss,
As thunder louder than your own made rock
The orbèd world—if then my words had power,
Though I am changed so that aught evil wish   70
Is dead within; although no memory be
Of what is hate—let them not lose it now!
What was that curse? for ye all heard me speak.

First Voice, from the Mountains
Thrice three hundred thousand years
    O'er the Earthquake's couch we stood: 75
Oft, as men convulsed with fears,
    We trembled in our multitude.

Second Voice, from the Springs

Thunderbolts had parched our water,
  We had been stained with bitter blood,
And had run mute, mid shrieks of slaughter,   80
  Through a city and a solitude.

Third Voice, from the Air

I had clothed, since Earth uprose,
  Its wastes in colours not their own;
And oft had my serene repose
  Been cloven by many a rending groan.   85

Fourth Voice, from the Whirlwinds

We had soared beneath these mountains
  Unresting ages; nor had thunder,
Nor yon Volcano's flaming fountains,
  Nor any power above or under
Ever made us mute with wonder.   90

First Voice

But never bowed our snowy crest
As at the voice of thine unrest.

Second Voice

Never such a sound before
To the Indian waves we bore.
A pilot asleep on the howling sea   95
Leaped up from the deck in agony
And heard, and cried, 'Ah, woe is me!'
And died as mad as the wild waves be.

Third Voice

By such dread words from Earth to Heaven
My still realm was never riven: 100
When its wound was closed, there stood
Darkness o'er the day like blood.

Fourth Voice

And we shrank back: for dreams of ruin
To frozen caves our flight pursuing
Made us keep silence—thus—and thus—   105
Though silence is as hell to us.

The Earth The tongueless caverns of the craggy hills
  Cried, 'Misery!' then the hollow Heaven replied,
  'Misery!' and the Ocean's purple waves,
  Climbing the land, howled to the lashing winds,   110
  And the pale nations heard it,—'Misery!'

Prometheus I hear a sound of voices: not the voice
  Which I gave forth. Mother, thy sons and thou
  Scorn him, without whose all-enduring will
  Beneath the fierce omnipotence of Jove,   115
  Both they and thou had vanished like thin mist
  Unrolled on the morning wind. Know ye not me,
  The Titan? he who made his agony
  The barrier to your else all-conquering foe?
  O rock-embosomed lawns, and snow-fed streams,   120
  Now seen athwart frore vapours, deep below,
  Through whose o'ershadowing woods I wandered once
  With Asia, drinking life from her loved eyes,
  Why scorns the spirit which informs ye, now
  To commune with me? me alone, who checked—   125
  As one who checks a fiend-drawn charioteer—

The falsehood and the force of Him who reigns
Supreme, and with the groans of pining slaves
Fills your dim glens and liquid wildernesses?
Why answer ye not, still? Brethren!   130

The Earth   They dare not.

Prometheus Who dares? For I would hear that curse
    again. . . .
    Ha, what an awful whisper rises up!
    'Tis scarce like sound: it tingles through the frame
    As lightning tingles, hovering ere it strike—
    Speak, Spirit! from thine inorganic voice   135
    I only know that thou art moving near
    And love. How cursed I him?

The Earth   How canst thou hear,
    Who knowest not the language of the dead?

Prometheus Thou art a living spirit; speak as they.

The Earth I dare not speak like life, lest Heaven's fell King   140
    Should hear, and link me to some wheel of pain
    More torturing than the one whereon I roll.
    Subtle thou art and good; and though the Gods
    Hear not this voice, yet thou art more than God
    Being wise and kind: earnestly hearken now.   145

Prometheus Obscurely through my brain, like shadows dim,
    Sweep awful thoughts, rapid and thick—I feel
    Faint, like one mingled in entwining love.
    Yet 'tis not pleasure.

The Earth   No, thou canst not hear:
 Thou art immortal, and this tongue is known   150
 Only to those who die. . . .

Prometheus   And what art thou,
 O melancholy Voice?

The Earth   I am the Earth
 Thy mother, she within whose stony veins,
 To the last fibre of the loftiest tree
 Whose thin leaves trembled in the frozen air,   155
 Joy ran, as blood within a living frame,
 When thou didst from her bosom, like a beam
 From sunrise, leap—a spirit of keen joy!
 And at thy voice her pining sons uplifted
 Their prostrate brows from the polluting dust,   160
 And our almighty Tyrant with fierce dread
 Grew pale—until his thunder chained thee here.
 Then—see those million worlds which burn and roll
 Around us: their inhabitants beheld
 My spherèd light wane in wide Heaven; the sea   165
 Was lifted with strange tempest, and new fire
 From earthquake-rifted mountains of bright snow
 Shook its portentous hair beneath Heaven's frown;
 Lightning and Inundation vexed the plains;
 Blue thistles bloomed in cities; foodless toads   170
 Within voluptuous chambers panting crawled;
 When Plague had fallen on man and beast and worm,
 And Famine, and black blight on herb and tree;
 And in the corn, and vines, and meadow-grass,
 Teemed ineradicable poisonous weeds   175
 Draining their growth, for my wan breast was dry
 With grief; and the thin air, my breath, was stained

With the contagion of a mother's hate
Breathed on her child's destroyer—aye, I heard
Thy curse, the which, if thou rememberest not,   180
Yet my innumerable seas and streams,
Mountains, and caves, and winds, and yon wide air,
And the inarticulate people of the dead,
Preserve, a treasured spell. We meditate
In secret joy and hope those dreadful words,   185
But dare not speak them.

Prometheus   Venerable Mother!
All else who live and suffer take from thee
Some comfort; flowers, and fruits, and happy sounds,
And love, though fleeting; these may not be mine.
But mine own words, I pray, deny me not.   190

The Earth They shall be told. Ere Babylon was dust,
The Magus Zoroaster, my dead child,
Met his own image walking in the garden.
That apparition, sole of men, he saw.
For know there are two worlds of life and death: 195
One that which thou beholdest; but the other
Is underneath the grave, where do inhabit
The shadows of all forms that think and live
Till death unite them and they part no more;
Dreams and the light imaginings of men,   200
And all that faith creates or love desires,
Terrible, strange, sublime and beauteous shapes.
There thou art, and dost hang, a writhing shade
Mid whirlwind-shaken mountains; all the Gods
Are there, and all the Powers of nameless worlds,   205
Vast, sceptred Phantoms; heroes, men, and beasts;
And Demogorgon, a tremendous Gloom;

And he, the Supreme Tyrant, throned
On burning gold. Son, one of these shall utter
The curse which all remember. Call at will   210
Thine own ghost, or the ghost of Jupiter,
Hades, or Typhon, or what mightier Gods
From all-prolific evil, since thy ruin
Have sprung, and trampled on my prostrate sons—
Ask, and they must reply: so the revenge   215
Of the Supreme may sweep through vacant shades,
As rainy wind through the abandoned gate
Of a fallen palace.

Prometheus   Mother, let not aught
  Of that which may be evil, pass again
  My lips, or those of aught resembling me—   220
  Phantasm of Jupiter, arise, appear!

Ione

  My wings are folded o'er mine ears:
    My wings are crossed over mine eyes:
  Yet through their silver shade appears,
    And through their lulling plumes arise,   225
      A Shape, a throng of sounds;
      May it be no ill to thee
      O thou of many wounds!
  Near whom, for our sweet sister's sake,
  Ever thus we watch and wake.   230

Panthea

  The sound is of whirlwind underground,
    Earthquake, and fire, and mountains cloven;
  The Shape is awful like the sound,
    Clothed in dark purple, star-inwoven.

A sceptre of pale gold 235
   To stay steps proud o'er the slow cloud
  His veinèd hand doth hold.
Cruel he looks, but calm and strong,
Like one who does, not suffers, wrong.

Phantasm of Jupiter Why have the secret powers of this
   strange world 240
  Driven me, a frail and empty phantom, hither
  On direst storms? What unaccustomed sounds
  Are hovering on my lips, unlike the voice
  With which our pallid race hold ghastly talk
  In darkness? And, proud Sufferer, who art thou? 245

Prometheus Tremendous Image, as thou art must be
  He whom thou shadowest forth. I am his foe,
  The Titan. Speak the words which I would hear,
  Although no thought inform thine empty voice.

The Earth Listen! And though your echoes must be mute, 250
  Grey mountains, and old woods, and haunted springs,
  Prophetic caves, and isle-surrounding streams,
  Rejoice to hear what yet ye cannot speak.

Phantasm A spirit seizes me and speaks within:
  It tears me as fire tears a thunder-cloud. 255

Panthea See, how he lifts his mighty looks, the Heaven
  Darkens above.

Ione   He speaks! O shelter me!

Prometheus I see the curse on gestures proud and cold,
   And looks of firm defiance, and calm hate,
   And such despair as mocks itself with smiles,   260
   Written as on a scroll . . . yet speak—O speak!

Phantasm

   Fiend, I defy thee! with a calm, fixed mind,
      All that thou canst inflict I bid thee do;
   Foul Tyrant both of Gods and Humankind,
      One only being shalt thou not subdue.   265
         Rain then thy plagues upon me here,
         Ghastly disease, and frenzying fear;
         And let alternate frost and fire
         Eat into me, and be thine ire
   Lightning, and cutting hail, and legioned forms   270
   Of furies, driving by upon the wounding storms.

   Aye, do thy worst. Thou art Omnipotent.
      O'er all things but thyself I gave thee power,
   And my own will. Be thy swift mischiefs sent
      To blast mankind, from yon etherial tower.   275
         Let thy malignant spirit move
         Its darkness over those I love:
         On me and mine I imprecate
         The utmost torture of thy hate;
   And thus devote to sleepless agony   280
   This undeclining head while thou must reign on high.

   But thou who art the God and Lord—O thou
      Who fillest with thy soul this world of woe,
   To whom all things of Earth and Heaven do bow
      In fear and worship—all-prevailing foe!   285

I curse thee! let a sufferer's curse
Clasp thee, his torturer, like remorse,
Till thine Infinity shall be
A robe of envenomed agony,
And thine Omnipotence a crown of pain   290
To cling like burning gold round thy dissolving brain.

Heap on thy soul by virtue of this Curse
  Ill deeds, then be thou damned, beholding good;
Both infinite as is this Universe,
  And thou, and thy self-torturing solitude.   295
    An awful Image of calm power
    Though now thou sittest, let the hour
    Come, when thou must appear to be
    That which thou art internally,
And after many a false and fruitless crime   300
Scorn track thy lagging fall through boundless space
    and time.

Prometheus Were these my words, O Parent?

The Earth   They were thine.

Prometheus It doth repent me: words are quick and vain;
  Grief for awhile is blind, and so was mine.
    I wish no living thing to suffer pain.   305

The Earth Misery, O misery to me
          That Jove at length should vanquish thee.
          Wail, howl aloud, Land and Sea,
          The Earth's rent heart shall answer ye.
    Howl, Spirits of the living and the dead,   310
    Your refuge, your defence lies fallen and vanquishèd.

First Echo

Lies fallen and vanquishèd?

Second Echo

Fallen and vanquishèd!

Ione

Fear not: 'tis but some passing spasm,
The Titan is unvanquished still.   315
But see, where through the azure chasm
Of yon forked and snowy hill
Trampling the slant winds on high
With golden-sandalled feet, that glow
Under plumes of purple dye,   320
Like rose-ensanguined ivory,
    A Shape comes now,
Stretching on high from his right hand
    A serpent-cinctured wand.

Panthea

'Tis Jove's world-wandering herald, Mercury.   325

Ione

And who are those with hydra tresses
And iron wings that climb the wind,
Whom the frowning God represses
Like vapours steaming up behind,
Clanging loud, an endless crowd—   330

Panthea

These are Jove's tempest-walking hounds,
Whom he gluts with groans and blood,
When charioted on sulphurous cloud
    He bursts Heaven's bounds.

Ione
Are they now led from the thin dead 335
On new pangs to be fed?

Panthea The Titan looks as ever, firm, not proud.

First Fury Ha! I scent life!

Second Fury Let me but look into his eyes!

Third Fury The hope of torturing him smells like a heap
Of corpses to a death-bird after battle. 340

First Fury Darest thou delay, O Herald? take cheer, Hounds
Of Hell—what if the Son of Maia soon
Should make us food and sport? Who can please long
The Omnipotent?

Mercury Back to your towers of iron,
And gnash, beside the streams of fire and wail, 345
Your foodless teeth! . . . Geryon, arise! and Gorgon,
Chimaera, and thou Sphinx, subtlest of fiends,
Who ministered to Thebes Heaven's poisoned wine,
Unnatural love, and more unnatural hate:
These shall perform your task.

First Fury O mercy! mercy! 350
We die with our desire—drive us not back!

Mercury Crouch then in silence.—Awful Sufferer,
To thee unwilling, most unwillingly
I come, by the great Father's will driven down
To execute a doom of new revenge. 355

Alas, I pity thee, and hate myself
That I can do no more—aye from thy sight
Returning, for a season heaven seems hell,
So thy worn form pursues me night and day,
Smiling reproach. Wise art thou, firm and good,   360
But vainly wouldst stand forth alone in strife
Against the Omnipotent; as yon clear lamps
That measure and divide the weary years
From which there is no refuge, long have taught
And long must teach. Even now thy Torturer arms   365
With the strange might of unimagined pains
The powers who scheme slow agonies in Hell,
And my commission is to lead them here,
Or what more subtle, foul, and savage fiends
People the abyss, and leave them to their task.   370
Be it not so . . . there is a secret known
To thee and to none else of living things
Which may transfer the sceptre of wide Heaven,
The fear of which perplexes the Supreme:
Clothe it in words, and bid it clasp his throne   375
In intercession; bend thy soul in prayer,
And like a suppliant in some gorgeous fane
Let the will kneel within thy haughty heart:
For benefits and meek submission tame
The fiercest and the mightiest.   380

Prometheus   Evil minds
Change good to their own nature. I gave all
He has; and in return he chains me here
Years, ages, night and day: whether the Sun
Split my parched skin, or in the moony night
The crystal-wingèd snow cling round my hair—   385
Whilst my belovèd race is trodden down

By his thought-executing ministers.
Such is the tyrant's recompense—'tis just:
He who is evil can receive no good;
And for a world bestowed, or a friend lost,   390
He can feel hate, fear, shame—not gratitude:
He but requites me for his own misdeed.
Kindness to such is keen reproach, which breaks
With bitter stings the light sleep of Revenge.
Submission, thou dost know, I cannot try: 395
For what submission but that fatal word,
The death-seal of mankind's captivity,
Like the Sicilian's hair-suspended sword
Which trembles o'er his crown, would he accept
Or could I yield?—which yet I will not yield.   400
Let others flatter Crime where it sits throned
In brief Omnipotence; secure are they:
For Justice when triumphant will weep down
Pity, not punishment, on her own wrongs,
Too much avenged by those who err. I wait,   405
Enduring thus, the retributive hour
Which since we spake is even nearer now—
But hark, the hell-hounds clamour: fear delay:
Behold! Heaven lowers under thy Father's frown.

Mercury O that we might be spared—I to inflict,   410
   And thou to suffer! Once more answer me:
   Thou knowest not the period of Jove's power?

Prometheus I know but this, that it must come.

Mercury   Alas,
   Thou canst not count thy years to come of pain?

Prometheus They last while Jove must reign: nor more, nor
    less   415
  Do I desire or fear.

Mercury   Yet pause, and plunge
  Into Eternity, where recorded time,
  Even all that we imagine, age on age,
  Seems but a point, and the reluctant mind
  Flags wearily in its unending flight   420
  Till it sink, dizzy, blind, lost, shelterless;
  Perchance it has not numbered the slow years
  Which thou must spend in torture, unreprieved.

Prometheus Perchance no thought can count them—yet
  they pass.

Mercury If thou might'st dwell among the Gods the while, 425
  Lapped in voluptuous joy?

Prometheus   I would not quit
  This bleak ravine, these unrepentant pains.

Mercury Alas! I wonder at, yet pity thee.

Prometheus Pity the self-despising slaves of Heaven,
  Not me, within whose mind sits peace serene   430
  As light in the sun, throned. . . . How vain is talk!
  Call up the fiends.

Ione   O sister, look! White fire
  Has cloven to the roots yon huge snow-loaded cedar;
  How fearfully God's thunder howls behind!

Mercury I must obey his words and thine—alas!   435
   Most heavily remorse hangs at my heart!

Panthea See where the child of Heaven with wingèd feet
   Runs down the slanted sunlight of the dawn.

Ione Dear sister, close thy plumes over thine eyes
   Lest thou behold and die—they come, they come   440
   Blackening the birth of day with countless wings,
   And hollow underneath, like death.

First Fury   Prometheus!

Second Fury Immortal Titan!

Third Fury   Champion of Heaven's slaves!

Prometheus He whom some dreadful voice invokes is here,
   Prometheus, the chained Titan. Horrible forms,   445
   What and who are ye? Never yet there came
   Phantasms so foul through monster-teeming Hell
   From the all-miscreative brain of Jove;
   Whilst I behold such execrable shapes
   Methinks I grow like what I contemplate,   450
   And laugh and stare in loathsome sympathy.

First Fury We are the ministers of pain and fear,
   And disappointment, and mistrust, and hate,
   And clinging crime; and as lean dogs pursue
   Through wood and lake some struck and sobbing fawn, 455
   We track all things that weep, and bleed, and live,
   When the great King betrays them to our will.

Prometheus O many fearful natures in one name,
  I know ye, and these lakes and echoes know
  The darkness and the clangour of your wings.   460
  But why more hideous than your loathèd selves
  Gather ye up in legions from the deep?

Second Fury We knew not that: Sisters, rejoice, rejoice!

Prometheus Can aught exult in its deformity?

Second Fury The beauty of delight makes lovers glad,   465
  Gazing on one another: so are we.
  As from the rose which the pale priestess kneels
  To gather for her festal crown of flowers
  The aërial crimson falls, flushing her cheek,
  So from our victim's destined agony   470
  The shade which is our form invests us round,
  Else are we shapeless as our mother Night.

Prometheus I laugh your power, and his who sent you here,
  To lowest scorn.—Pour forth the cup of pain.

First Fury Thou thinkest we will rend thee bone from bone, 475
  And nerve from nerve, working like fire within?

Prometheus Pain is my element, as hate is thine;
  Ye rend me now: I care not.

Second Fury   Dost imagine
  We will but laugh into thy lidless eyes?

Prometheus I weigh not what ye do, but what ye suffer,   480
  Being evil. Cruel was the Power which called
  You, or aught else so wretched, into light.

Third Fury Thou think'st we will live through thee, one by
    one,
    Like animal life, and though we can obscure not
    The soul which burns within, that we will dwell   485
    Beside it, like a vain loud multitude
    Vexing the self-content of wisest men:
    That we will be dread thought beneath thy brain,
    And foul desire round thine astonished heart,
    And blood within thy labyrinthine veins   490
    Crawling like agony?

Prometheus   Why, ye are thus now;
    Yet am I king over myself, and rule
    The torturing and conflicting throngs within,
    As Jove rules you when Hell grows mutinous.

Chorus of Furies

    From the ends of the Earth, from the ends of the Earth 495
    Where the night has its grave and the morning its birth,
          Come, come, come!
    O ye who shake hills with the scream of your mirth
    When cities sink howling in ruin; and ye
    Who with wingless footsteps trample the Sea,   500
    And close upon Shipwreck and Famine's track
    Sit chattering with joy on the foodless wreck;
          Come, come, come!
      Leave the bed, low, cold, and red,
      Strewed beneath a nation dead;   505
      Leave the hatred—as in ashes
      Fire is left for future burning,
      It will burst in bloodier flashes
      When ye stir it, soon returning;

Leave the self-contempt implanted   510
In young spirits sense-enchanted,
Misery's yet unkindled fuel;
Leave Hell's secrets half-unchanted
To the maniac dreamer: cruel
More than ye can be with hate   515
    Is he with fear.
    Come, come, come!
We are steaming up from Hell's wide gate,
And we burthen the blasts of the atmosphere,
But vainly we toil till ye come here.   520

Ione Sister, I hear the thunder of new wings.

Panthea These solid mountains quiver with the sound
  Even as the tremulous air: their shadows make
  The space within my plumes more black than night.

First Fury

Your call was as a wingèd car   525
Driven on whirlwinds fast and far;
It rapt us from red gulfs of war.

Second Fury

From wide cities famine-wasted—

Third Fury

Groans half heard, and blood untasted—

Fourth Fury

Kingly conclaves stern and cold   530
Where blood with gold is bought and sold;

Fifth Fury

From the furnace white and hot
In which—

A Fury

Speak not—whisper not:
I know all that ye would tell,
But to speak might break the spell   535
Which must bend the Invincible,
    The stern of thought;
He yet defies the deepest power of Hell.

A Fury

Tear the veil!

Another Fury

It is torn!

Chorus

The pale stars of the morn
Shine on a misery dire to be borne.   540
Dost thou faint, mighty Titan? We laugh thee to scorn.
Dost thou boast the clear knowledge thou waken'dst
   for man?
Then was kindled within him a thirst which outran
Those perishing waters; a thirst of fierce fever,
Hope, love, doubt, desire—which consume him for ever. 545
    One came forth of gentle worth
    Smiling on the sanguine earth;
    His words outlived him, like swift poison
    Withering up truth, peace, and pity.
    Look where round the wide horizon   550
    Many a million-peopled city

Vomits smoke in the bright air—
Hark that outcry of despair!
'Tis his mild and gentle ghost
Wailing for the faith he kindled: 555
Look again, the flames almost
To a glow-worm's lamp have dwindled:
The survivors round the embers
   Gather in dread.
      Joy, joy, joy!   560
Past ages crowd on thee, but each one remembers;
And the future is dark, and the present is spread
Like a pillow of thorns for thy slumberless head.

Semichorus I

Drops of bloody agony flow
From his white and quivering brow.   565
Grant a little respite now—
See, a disenchanted Nation
Springs like day from desolation;
To Truth its state is dedicate,
And Freedom leads it forth, her mate;   570
A legioned band of linkèd brothers
Whom Love calls children—

Semichorus II

      'Tis another's—
See how kindred murder kin!
'Tis the vintage-time for Death and Sin:
Blood, like new wine, bubbles within;   575
   Till Despair smothers
The struggling World—which slaves and tyrants win.

      [*All the Furies vanish, except one*

Ione Hark, sister! what a low yet dreadful groan
    Quite unsuppressed is tearing up the heart
    Of the good Titan, as storms tear the deep,   580
    And beasts hear the sea moan in inland caves.
    Darest thou observe how the fiends torture him?

Panthea Alas, I looked forth twice, but will no more.

Ione What didst thou see?

Panthea   A woeful sight—a youth
    With patient looks nailed to a crucifix.   585

Ione What next?

Panthea   The Heaven around, the Earth below
    Was peopled with thick shapes of human death,
    All horrible, and wrought by human hands,
    Though some appeared the work of human hearts,
    For men were slowly killed by frowns and smiles: 590
    And other sights too foul to speak and live
    Were wandering by—let us not tempt worse fear
    By looking forth: those groans are grief enough.

Fury Behold, an emblem: those who do endure
    Deep wrongs for man, and scorn, and chains, but heap   595
    Thousandfold torment on themselves and him.

Prometheus Remit the anguish of that lighted stare;
    Close those wan lips; let that thorn-wounded brow
    Stream not with blood—it mingles with thy tears!
    Fix, fix those tortured orbs in peace and death,   600
    So thy sick throes shake not that crucifix,

So those pale fingers play not with thy gore.
O, horrible! Thy name I will not speak,
It hath become a curse. I see, I see
The wise, the mild, the lofty, and the just,   605
Whom thy slaves hate for being like to thee,
Some hunted by foul lies from their heart's home,
An early-chosen, late-lamented home,
As hooded ounces cling to the driven hind;
Some linked to corpses in unwholesome cells: 610
Some—hear I not the multitude laugh loud?—
Impaled in lingering fire: and mighty realms
Float by my feet like sea-uprooted isles,
Whose sons are kneaded down in common blood
By the red light of their own burning homes—   615

Fury Blood thou canst see, and fire; and canst hear groans;
  Worse things unheard, unseen, remain behind.

Prometheus Worse?

Fury   In each human heart terror survives
  The ravin it has gorged: the loftiest fear
  All that they would disdain to think were true: 620
  Hypocrisy and custom make their minds
  The fanes of many a worship, now outworn.
  They dare not devise good for man's estate,
  And yet they know not that they do not dare.
  The good want power, but to weep barren tears.   625
  The powerful goodness want: worse need for them.
  The wise want love, and those who love want wisdom;
  And all best things are thus confused to ill.
  Many are strong and rich,—and would be just—
  But live among their suffering fellow men   630
  As if none felt: they know not what they do.

Prometheus Thy words are like a cloud of wingèd snakes;
   And yet I pity those they torture not.

Fury Thou pitiest them? I speak no more!

                        [*Vanishes*
Prometheus   Ah woe!
   Ah woe! Alas! pain, pain ever, forever?   635
   I close my tearless eyes, but see more clear
   Thy works within my woe-illumèd mind,
   Thou subtle tyrant . . . . Peace is in the grave—
   The grave hides all things beautiful and good:
   I am a God and cannot find it there—   640
   Nor would I seek it. For, though dread revenge,
   This is defeat, fierce King, not victory!
   The sights with which thou torturest gird my soul
   With new endurance, till the hour arrives
   When they shall be no types of things which are.   645

Panthea Alas! what sawest thou more?

Prometheus   There are two woes:
   To speak, and to behold; thou spare me one.
   Names are there, Nature's sacred watchwords—they
   Were borne aloft in bright emblazonry;
   The nations thronged around, and cried aloud   650
   As with one voice, 'Truth, Liberty, and Love!'
   Suddenly fierce confusion fell from Heaven
   Among them—there was strife, deceit, and fear;
   Tyrants rushed in, and did divide the spoil.
   This was the shadow of the truth I saw.   655

The Earth I felt thy torture, Son, with such mixed joy
   As pain and Virtue give. To cheer thy state

I bid ascend those subtle and fair spirits
Whose homes are the dim caves of human thought,
And who inhabit, as birds wing the wind,   660
Its world-surrounding ether: they behold
Beyond that twilight realm, as in a glass,
The future: may they speak comfort to thee!

Panthea Look, Sister, where a troop of spirits gather,
 Like flocks of clouds in spring's delightful weather, 665
 Thronging in the blue air!

Ione   And see! more come,
 Like fountain-vapours when the winds are dumb,
 That climb up the ravine in scattered lines.
 And hark! is it the music of the pines?
 Is it the lake? Is it the waterfall?   670

Panthea 'Tis something sadder, sweeter far than all.

Chorus of Spirits

 From unremembered ages we
 Gentle guides and guardians be
 Of Heaven-oppressed mortality;
 And we breathe, and sicken not,   675
 The atmosphere of human thought:
 Be it dim and dank and grey
 Like a storm-extinguished day
 Travelled o'er by dying gleams;
 Be it bright as all between   680
 Cloudless skies and windless streams,
 Silent, liquid, and serene—
 As the birds within the wind,
 As the fish within the wave,

As the thoughts of man's own mind 685
Float through all above the grave,
We make there our liquid lair,
Voyaging cloudlike and unpent
Through the boundless element—
Thence we bear the prophecy 690
Which begins and ends in thee!

Ione More yet come, one by one: the air around them
Looks radiant, like the air around a star.

First Spirit

On a battle-trumpet's blast
I fled hither, fast, fast, fast, 695
Mid the darkness upward cast—
From the dust of creeds outworn,
From the tyrant's banner torn,
Gathering round me, onward borne,
There was mingled many a cry— 700
Freedom! Hope! Death! Victory!
Till they faded through the sky
And one sound above, around,
One sound beneath, around, above,
Was moving; 'twas the soul of love; 705
'Twas the hope, the prophecy
Which begins and ends in thee.

Second Spirit

A rainbow's arch stood on the sea
Which rocked beneath, immoveably;
And the triumphant Storm did flee 710
Like a conqueror swift and proud

Between, with many a captive cloud,
A shapeless, dark and rapid crowd,
Each by lightning riven in half:
I heard the thunder hoarsely laugh: 715
Mighty fleets were strewn like chaff
And spread beneath a hell of death
O'er the white waters. I alit
On a great ship lightning-split,
And speeded hither on the sigh   720
Of one who gave an enemy
His plank—then plunged aside to die.

Third Spirit

I sat beside a sage's bed,
And the lamp was burning red
Near the book where he had fed,   725
When a Dream with plumes of flame
To his pillow hovering came,
And I knew it was the same
Which had kindled long ago
Pity, eloquence, and woe;   730
And the world awhile below
Wore the shade its lustre made.
It has borne me here as fleet
As Desire's lightning feet:
I must ride it back ere morrow,   735
Or the sage will wake in sorrow.

Fourth Spirit

On a Poet's lips I slept
Dreaming like a love-adept
In the sound his breathing kept;

Nor seeks nor finds he mortal blisses, 740
But feeds on the aërial kisses
Of shapes that haunt thought's wildernesses.
He will watch from dawn to gloom
The lake-reflected sun illume
The yellow bees i' the ivy-bloom, 745
Nor heed nor see what things they be;
But from these create he can
Forms more real than living man,
Nurslings of immortality!—
One of these awakened me, 750
And I sped to succour thee.

Ione Behold'st thou not two shapes from the east and west
Come, as two doves to one belovèd nest,
Twin nurslings of the all-sustaining air
On swift still wings glide down the atmosphere? 755
And hark! their sweet sad voices; 'tis despair
Mingled with love, and then dissolved in sound.

Panthea Canst thou speak, sister? all my words are drowned.

Ione Their beauty gives me voice. See how they float
On their sustaining wings of skiey grain, 760
Orange and azure deepening into gold:
Their soft smiles light the air like a star's fire.

Chorus of Spirits
Hast thou beheld the form of Love?

Fifth Spirit
As over wide dominions
I sped, like some swift cloud that wings the wide
air's wildernesses,

That planet-crested Shape swept by on lightning-
  braided pinions,   765
    Scattering the liquid joy of life from his ambrosial
      tresses:
His footsteps paved the world with light—but as I passed
  'twas fading,
    And hollow Ruin yawned behind: great Sages bound
      in madness,
And headless patriots, and pale youths who perished
  unupbraiding
    Gleamed in the Night I wandered o'er—till thou, O
      King of sadness,   770
    Turned by thy smile the worst I saw to recollected
      gladness.

Sixth Spirit

Ah sister, Desolation is a delicate thing:
  It walks not on the Earth, it floats not on the air,
But treads with lulling footstep, and fans with silent
  wing
    The tender hopes which in their hearts the best and
      gentlest bear,   775
Who, soothed to false repose by the fanning plumes
  above,
    And the music-stirring motion of its soft and busy
      feet,
Dream visions of aërial joy, and call the monster Love,
  And wake, and find the shadow Pain—as he whom
    now we greet.

Chorus

        Though Ruin now Love's shadow be,   780
        Following him destroyingly

On Death's white and wingèd steed
Which the fleetest cannot flee—
Trampling down both flower and weed,
Man and beast, and foul and fair,   785
Like a tempest through the air;
Thou shalt quell this Horseman grim,
Woundless though in heart or limb.

Prometheus Spirits! how know ye this shall be?

Chorus

In the atmosphere we breathe,   790
As buds grow red when snow-storms flee,
From spring gathering up beneath,
Whose mild winds shake the elder brake,
And the wandering herdsmen know
That the white-thorn soon will blow: 795
Wisdom, Justice, Love, and Peace,
When they struggle to increase,
Are to us as soft winds be
To shepherd-boys—the prophecy
Which begins and ends in thee.   800

Ione Where are the Spirits fled?

Panthea   Only a sense
Remains of them, like the omnipotence
Of music, when the inspired voice and lute
Languish, ere yet the responses are mute
Which through the deep and labyrinthine soul,   805
Like echoes through long caverns, wind and roll.

Prometheus How fair these air-born shapes! and yet I feel
Most vain all hope but love; and thou art far,

Asia! who, when my being overflowed,
Wert like a golden chalice to bright wine   810
Which else had sunk into the thirsty dust.
All things are still: alas! how heavily
This quiet morning weighs upon my heart;
Though I should dream, I could even sleep with grief
If slumber were denied not . . . I would fain   815
Be what it is my destiny to be,
The saviour and the strength of suffering man,
Or sink into the original gulf of things . . .
There is no agony, and no solace left;
Earth can console, Heaven can torment no more.   820

Panthea Hast thou forgotten one who watches thee
The cold dark night, and never sleeps but when
The shadow of thy spirit falls on her?

Prometheus I said all hope was vain but love: thou lovest.

Panthea Deeply in truth; but the Eastern star looks white,   825
And Asia waits in that far Indian vale
The scene of her sad exile—rugged once
And desolate and frozen like this ravine;
But now invested with fair flowers and herbs,
And haunted by sweet airs and sounds, which flow   830
Among the woods and waters, from the ether
Of her transforming presence—which would fade
If it were mingled not with thine. Farewell!

End of the First Act

From Act II, Scene ii
Written spring 1819

Semichorus I of Spirits

The path through which that lovely twain
Have passed, by cedar, pine, and yew,
And each dark tree that ever grew,
Is curtained out from Heaven's wide blue;
Nor sun, nor moon, nor wind, nor rain   5
Can pierce its interwoven bowers,
Nor aught, save where some cloud of dew,
Drifted along the earth-creeping breeze
Between the trunks of the hoar trees,
Hangs each a pearl in the pale flowers   10
Of the green laurel, blown anew;
And bends, and then fades silently,
One frail and fair anemone:
Or where some star of many a one
That climb and wander through steep Night,   15
Has found the cleft through which alone
Beams fall from high those depths upon,
Ere it is borne away, away,
By the swift Heavens that cannot stay—
It scatters drops of golden light,   20
Like lines of rain that ne'er unite:
And the gloom divine is all around;
And underneath is the mossy ground.

Semichorus II

There the voluptuous nightingales
Are awake through all the broad noonday;   25
When one with bliss or sadness fails,

And through the windless ivy-boughs,
Sick with sweet love, droops dying away
On its mate's music-panting bosom—
Another from the swinging blossom,   30
Watching to catch the languid close
Of the last strain, then lifts on high
The wings of the weak melody,
Till some new stream of feeling bear
The song, and all the woods are mute;   35
When there is heard through the dim air
The rush of wings, and rising there
Like many a lake-surrounded flute,
Sounds overflow the listener's brain
So sweet, that joy is almost pain.   40

Semichorus I

There those enchanted eddies play
Of echoes music-tongued, which draw,
By Demogorgon's mighty law,
With melting rapture, or sweet awe,
All spirits on that secret way,   45
As inland boats are driven to Ocean
Down streams made strong with mountain-thaw;
And first there comes a gentle sound
To those in talk or slumber bound,
And wakes the destined: soft emotion   50
Attracts, impels them; those who saw
Say from the breathing Earth behind
There steams a plume-uplifting wind
Which drives them on their path, while they
Believe their own swift wings and feet   55
The sweet desires within obey:
And so they float upon their way

Until, still sweet, but loud and strong,
The storm of sound is driven along,
Sucked up and hurrying: as they fleet   60
Behind, its gathering billows meet
And to the fatal mountain bear
Like clouds amid the yielding air.

From Act II, Scene v

Voice in the Air, Singing
Life of life! thy lips enkindle
With their love the breath between them;
And thy smiles before they dwindle
Make the cold air fire; then screen them
In those looks where whoso gazes   5
Faints, entangled in their mazes.

Child of Light! thy limbs are burning
Through the vest which seems to hide them,
As the radiant lines of morning
Through the clouds ere they divide them;   10
And this atmosphere divinest
Shrouds thee wheresoe'er thou shinest.

Fair are others;—none beholds thee,
But thy voice sounds low and tender
Like the fairest—for it folds thee   15
From the sight, that liquid splendour,
And all feel, yet see thee never,
As I feel now, lost forever!

Lamp of Earth! where'er thou movest
Its dim shapes are clad with brightness,   20
And the souls of whom thou lovest
Walk upon the winds with lightness,
Till they fail, as I am failing,
Dizzy, lost . . . yet unbewailing!

The Mask of Anarchy
written on the Occasion of the Massacre
at Manchester
Written September 1819. Published 1832

As I lay asleep in Italy
There came a voice from over the Sea,
And with great power it forth led me
To walk in the Visions of Poesy.

I met Murder on the way—   5
He had a mask like Castlereagh,
Very smooth he looked, yet grim;
Seven bloodhounds followed him:

All were fat, and well they might
Be in admirable plight,   10
For one by one and two by two
He tossed them human hearts to chew
Which from his wide cloak he drew.

Next came Fraud, and he had on
Like Eldon, an ermined gown;   15
His big tears, for he wept well,
Turned to millstones as they fell,

And the little children who
Round his feet played to and fro,
Thinking every tear a gem,   20
Had their brains knocked out by them.

Clothed with the Bible, as with light,
And the shadows of the night,
Like Sidmouth next, Hypocrisy
On a crocodile rode by.   25

And many more Destructions played
In this ghastly masquerade,
All disguised even to the eyes
Like Bishops, lawyers, peers and spies.

Last came Anarchy: he rode   30
On a white Horse, splashed with blood;
He was pale even to the lips
Like Death in the Apocalypse,

And he wore a kingly crown;
In his grasp a sceptre shone;   35
On his brow this mark I saw—
I AM GOD AND KING AND LAW.

With a pace stately and fast
Over English land he passed,
Trampling to a mire of blood   40
The adoring multitude.

And a mighty troop around
With their trampling shook the ground,
Waving each a bloody sword
For the service of their Lord,   45

And with glorious triumph they
Rode through England proud and gay,
Drunk as with intoxication
Of the wine of desolation.

O'er fields and towns, from sea to sea,   50
Passed that Pageant swift and free,
Tearing up and trampling down
Till they came to London town;

And each dweller, panic-stricken,
Felt his heart with terror sicken   55
Hearing the tempestuous cry
Of the triumph of Anarchy.

For with pomp to meet him came
Clothed in arms like blood and flame
The hired Murderers, who did sing   60
'Thou art God and Law and King.

'We have waited weak and lone
For thy coming, Mighty One!
Our purses are empty, our swords are cold,
Give us glory and blood and gold.'   65

Lawyers and priests, a motley crowd,
To the Earth their pale brows bowed,
Like a bad prayer not overloud
Whispering—'Thou art Law and God.'

Then all cried with one accord   70
'Thou art King and God and Lord;
Anarchy, to Thee we bow,
Be Thy name made holy now!'

And Anarchy, the Skeleton,
Bowed and grinned to every one   75
As well as if his education
Had cost ten millions to the Nation.

For he knew the Palaces
Of our Kings were rightly his;
His the sceptre, crown, and globe,   80
And the gold-inwoven robe.

So he sent his slaves before
To seize upon the Bank and Tower,
And was proceeding with intent
To meet his pensioned Parliament   85

When One fled past, a Maniac maid,
And her name was Hope, she said:
But she looked more like Despair,
And she cried out in the air—

'My Father Time is weak and grey   90
With waiting for a better day;
See how idiot-like he stands
Fumbling with his palsied hands.

He has had child after child
And the dust of death is piled   95
Over every one but me—
Misery, o Misery!'

Then she lay down in the street
Right before the horses' feet,
Expecting with a patient eye   100
Murder, Fraud and Anarchy.

When between her and her foes
A mist, a light, an image rose,
Small at first, and weak and frail
Like the vapour of a vale,   105

Till as clouds grow on the blast
Like tower-crowned giants striding fast,
And glare with lightnings as they fly
And speak in thunder to the sky,

It grew—a Shape arrayed in mail   110
Brighter than the Viper's scale,
And upborne on wings whose grain
Was as the light of sunny rain.

On its helm seen far away
A Planet, like the Morning's, lay;   115
And those plumes its light rained through
Like a shower of crimson dew;

With step as soft as wind it passed
O'er the heads of men—so fast
That they knew the presence there   120
And looked—but all was empty air.

As flowers beneath May's footstep waken,
As Stars from Night's loose hair are shaken,
As waves arise when loud winds call,
Thoughts sprung where'er that step did fall.   125

And the prostrate multitude
Looked—and ankle-deep in blood
Hope, that maiden most serene,
Was walking with a quiet mien,

And Anarchy, the ghastly birth,   130
Lay dead earth upon the earth;
The Horse of Death tameless as wind
Fled, and with his hoofs did grind
To dust the murderers thronged behind.

A rushing light of clouds and splendour,   135
A sense awakening and yet tender
Was heard and felt—and at its close
These words of joy and fear arose

As if their own indignant Earth
Which gave the Sons of England birth   140
Had felt their blood upon her brow,
And shuddering with a mother's throe

Had turned every drop of blood
By which her face had been bedewed
To an accent unwithstood—   145
As if her heart cried out aloud

'Men of England, Heirs of Glory,
Heroes of unwritten Story,
Nurslings of one mighty Mother,
Hopes of her and one another,   150

'Rise like Lions after slumber
In unvanquishable number,
Shake your chains to Earth like dew
Which in sleep had fallen on you—
Ye are many—they are few.   155

'What is Freedom?—ye can tell
That which slavery is, too well—
For its very name has grown
To an echo of your own:

''Tis to work and have such pay   160
As just keeps life from day to day
In your limbs, as in a cell
For the tyrants' use to dwell,

'So that ye for them are made
Loom and plough and sword and spade,   165
With or without your own will bent
To their defence and nourishment;

''Tis to see your children weak
With their mothers pine and peak
When the winter winds are bleak—   170
They are dying whilst I speak;

' 'Tis to hunger for such diet
As the rich man in his riot
Casts to the fat dogs that lie
Surfeiting beneath his eye;   175

''Tis to let the Ghost of Gold
Take from Toil a thousandfold
More than e'er its substance could
In the tyrannies of old—

'Paper coin, that forgery   180
Of the title deeds, which ye
Hold to something from the worth
Of the inheritance of Earth;

' ''Tis to be a slave in soul
And to hold no strong control   185
Over your own will, but be
All that others make of ye;

'And at length when ye complain
With a murmur weak and vain,
'Tis to see the tyrants' crew   190
Ride over your wives and you—
Blood is on the grass like dew.

'Then it is to feel revenge
Fiercely thirsting to exchange
Blood for blood, and wrong for wrong—   195
Do not thus when ye are strong.

'Birds find rest in narrow nest
When weary of their wingèd quest,
Beasts find fare in woody lair
When storm and snow are in the air;   200

'Horses, oxen, have a home
When from daily toil they come;
Household Dogs, when the wind roars
Find a home within warm doors;

'Asses, swine, have litter spread   205
And with fitting food are fed;
All things have a home but one—
Thou, o Englishman, hast none!

'This is slavery—savage men
Or wild beasts within a den   210
Would endure not as ye do—
But such ills they never knew.

'What art thou, Freedom? o, could slaves
Answer from their living graves
This demand, tyrants would flee   215
Like a dream's dim imagery.

'Thou art not as impostors say
A Shadow soon to pass away,
A Superstition, and a name
Echoing from the cave of Fame: 220

'For the labourer thou art bread
And a comely table spread,
From his daily labour come,
In a neat and happy home;

'Thou art clothes and fire and food   225
For the trampled multitude—
No—in countries that are free
Such starvation cannot be
As in England now we see.

'To the rich thou art a check—   230
When his foot is on the neck
Of his victim, thou dost make
That he treads upon a snake.

'Thou art Justice—ne'er for gold
May thy righteous laws be sold   235
As laws are in England—thou
Shieldst alike both high and low.

'Thou art Wisdom—Freeman never
Dream that God will damn forever
All who think those things untrue   240
Of which Priests make such ado—

'Thou art Peace—never by thee
Would blood and treasure wasted be
As tyrants wasted them, when all
Leagued to quench thy flame in Gaul.   245

'What if English toil and blood
Was poured forth even as a flood?
It availed, o Liberty,
To dim, but not extinguish thee.

'Thou art Love—the rich have kissed   250
Thy feet, and like him following Christ
Give their substance to the free
And through the rough world follow thee,

'Or turn their wealth to arms, and make
War for thy belovèd sake   255
On wealth and war and fraud—whence they
Drew the power which is their prey.

'Science, Poetry and Thought
Are thy lamps; they make the lot
Of the dwellers in a cot   260
Such, they curse their Maker not.

'Spirit, Patience, Gentleness,
All that can adorn and bless
Art thou . . . let deeds not words express
Thine exceeding loveliness—   265

'Let a great Assembly be
Of the fearless and the free
On some spot of English ground
Where the plains stretch wide around:

'Let the blue sky overhead,   270
The green earth on which ye tread,
All that must eternal be
Witness the Solemnity.

'From the corners uttermost
Of the bounds of English coast,   275
From every hut, village and town
Where those who live and suffer, moan
For others' misery or their own,

'From the Workhouse and the prison
Where pale as corpses newly risen   280
Women, children, young and old
Groan for pain and weep for cold—

'From the haunts of daily life
Where is waged the daily strife
With common wants and common cares   285
Which sows the human heart with tares—

'Lastly from the palaces
Where the murmur of distress
Echoes, like the distant sound
Of a wind alive around   290

'Those prison-halls of wealth and fashion
Where some few feel such compassion
For those who groan and toil and wail
As must make their brethren pale,

'Ye who suffer woes untold,   295
Or to feel or to behold
Your lost country bought and sold
With a price of blood and gold—

'Let a vast Assembly be,
And with great solemnity   300
Declare with measured words that ye
Are, as God has made ye, free—

'Be your strong and simple words
Keen to wound as sharpened swords,
And wide as targes let them be   305
With their shade to cover ye.

'Let the tyrants pour around
With a quick and startling sound
Like the loosening of a sea
Troops of armed emblazonry.   310

'Let the charged artillery drive
Till the dead air seems alive
With the clash of clanging wheels
And the tramp of horses' heels.

'Let the fixèd bayonet   315
Gleam with sharp desire to wet
Its bright point in English blood—
Looking keen, as one for food.

'Let the horsemen's scimitars
Wheel and flash like sphereless stars   320
Thirsting to eclipse their burning
In a sea of death and mourning.

'Stand ye calm and resolute
Like a forest close and mute
With folded arms and looks which are   325
Weapons of unvanquished War,

'And let Panic who outspeeds
The career of armed steeds
Pass, a disregarded shade,
Through your phalanx undismayed.   330

'Let the Laws of your own land,
Good or ill, between ye stand
Hand to hand and foot to foot,
Arbiters of the dispute,

'The old laws of England—they   335
Whose reverend heads with age are grey,
Children of a wiser day,
And whose solemn voice must be
Thine own echo—Liberty!

'On those who first should violate   340
Such sacred heralds in their state
Rest the blood that must ensue . . .
And it will not rest on you.

'And if then the tyrants dare
Let them ride among you there,   345
Slash and stab and maim and hew—
What they like that let them do.

'With folded arms, and steady eyes,
And little fear, and less surprise,
Look upon them as they slay   350
Till their rage has died away.

'Then they will return with shame
To the place from which they came,
And the blood thus shed will speak
In hot blushes on their cheek: 355

'Every Woman in the land
Will point at them as they stand . . .
They will hardly dare to greet
Their acquaintance in the street.

'And the bold, true warriors   360
Who have hugged Danger in wars
Will turn to those who would be free,
Ashamed of such base company.

'And that slaughter, to the Nation
Shall steam up like inspiration   365
Eloquent, oracular,—
A volcano heard afar,

'And these words shall then become
Like oppression's thundered doom
Ringing through each heart and brain,   370
Heard again, again, again,

'Rise like lions after slumber
In unvanquishable number,
Shake your chains to earth like dew
Which in sleep had fallen on you—   375
Ye are many—they are few—'

Ode to the West Wind

Written October 1819. *Prometheus Unbound* (1820)

I

O WILD West Wind, thou breath of Autumn's being,
Thou, from whose unseen presence the leaves dead
Are driven, like ghosts from an enchanter fleeing,

Yellow and black and pale and hectic red,
Pestilence-stricken multitudes: O Thou   5
Who chariotest to their dark wintry bed

The wingèd seeds, where they lie cold and low,
Each like a corpse within its grave, until
Thine azure sister of the Spring shall blow

Her clarion o'er the dreaming earth, and fill   10
(Driving sweet buds like flocks to feed in air)
With living hues and odours plain and hill:

Wild Spirit which art moving everywhere,
Destroyer and Preserver, hear, O hear!

II

Thou on whose stream, mid the steep sky's commotion,   15
Loose clouds like Earth's decaying leaves are shed,
Shook from the tangled boughs of Heaven and Ocean,

Angels of rain and lightning: there are spread
On the blue surface of thine aery surge,
Like the bright hair uplifted from the head   20

Of some fierce Maenad, even from the dim verge
Of the horizon to the zenith's height
The locks of the approaching storm. Thou dirge

Of the dying year, to which this closing night
Will be the dome of a vast sepulchre   25
Vaulted with all thy congregated might

Of vapours, from whose solid atmosphere
Black rain, and fire, and hail will burst: O, hear!

III

Thou who didst waken from his summer dreams
The blue Mediterranean, where he lay   30
Lulled by the coil of his crystalline streams,

Beside a pumice isle in Baiae's bay,
And saw in sleep old palaces and towers
Quivering within the wave's intenser day,

All overgrown with azure moss and flowers   35
So sweet, the sense faints picturing them! Thou
For whose path the Atlantic's level powers

Cleave themselves into chasms, while far below
The sea-blooms and the oozy woods which wear
The sapless foliage of the ocean, know   40

Thy voice, and suddenly grow grey with fear,
And tremble and despoil themselves: O, hear!

IV

If I were a dead leaf thou mightest bear—
If I were a swift cloud to fly with thee—
A wave to pant beneath thy power, and share   45

The impulse of thy strength, only less free
Than thou, O Uncontrollable! If even
I were as in my boyhood, and could be

The comrade of thy wanderings over Heaven,
As then, when to outstrip thy skiey speed   50
Scarce seemed a vision—I would ne'er have striven

As thus with thee in prayer in my sore need.
Oh! lift me as a wave, a leaf, a cloud!
I fall upon the thorns of life—I bleed—

A heavy weight of hours has chained and bowed   55
One too like thee: tameless, and swift, and proud.

V

Make me thy lyre, even as the forest is:
What if my leaves are falling like its own!
The tumult of thy mighty harmonies

Will take from both a deep, autumnal tone,   60
Sweet though in sadness. Be thou, Spirit fierce,
My spirit! Be thou me, impetuous one!

Drive my dead thoughts over the universe
Like withered leaves to quicken a new birth!
And, by the incantation of this verse,   65

Scatter, as from an unextinguished hearth
Ashes and sparks, my words among mankind!
Be through my lips to unawakened Earth

The trumpet of a prophecy! O Wind,
If Winter comes, can Spring be far behind?   70

Love's Philosophy

Written autumn 1819. Published 1819

THE fountains mingle with the river
   And the rivers with the ocean,
The winds of heaven mix forever
   With a sweet emotion;

Nothing in the world is single, 5
   All things by a law divine
In one spirit meet and mingle,
   Why not I with thine?—

See the mountains kiss high heaven
   And the waves clasp one another; 10
No sister flower would be forgiven
   If it disdained its brother,
And the sunlight clasps the earth
   And the moonbeams kiss the sea,
What is all this sweet work worth 15
   If thou kiss not me?

England in 1819

Written late 1819. Published 1839

An old, mad, blind, despised and dying King;
Princes, the dregs of their dull race, who flow
Through public scorn,—mud from a muddy spring;
Rulers who neither see nor feel nor know,
But leechlike to their fainting Country cling 5
Till they drop, blind in blood, without a blow;
A people starved and stabbed on the untilled field;
An army whom liberticide and prey
Makes as a two-edged sword to all who wield;
Golden and sanguine laws which tempt and slay; 10
Religion Christless, Godless, a book sealed;
A senate, Time's worst statute, unrepealed,
Are graves from which a glorious Phantom may
Burst, to illumine our tempestuous day.

Song
Written May 1820. Published 1824

RARELY, rarely comest thou,
   Spirit of Delight!
Wherefore hast thou left me now
   Many a day and night?
Many a weary night and day   5
'Tis since thou art fled away.

How shall ever one like me
   Win thee back again?
With the joyous and the free
   Thou wilt scoff at pain.   10
Spirit false! that hast forgot
All but those who need thee not.

As a lizard with the shade
   Of a trembling leaf,
Thou with sorrow art dismayed;   15
   Even the sighs of grief
Reproach thee, that thou art not near,
And reproach thou wilt not hear.

Let me set my mournful ditty
   To a merry measure;   20
Thou wilt never come for pity—
   Thou wilt come for pleasure,
Pity then will cut away
Those cruel wings, and thou wilt stay.

I love all that thou lovest,   25
   Spirit of Delight!
The fresh Earth in new leaves dressed,
   And the starry night,
Autumn evening, and the morn
When the golden mists are born.   30

I love snow, and all the forms
   Of the radiant frost;
I love waves and winds and storms—
   Every thing almost
Which is Nature's, and may be   35
Untainted by man's misery.

I love tranquil solitude,
   And such society
As is quiet, wise and good;
   Between thee and me   40
What difference? but thou dost possess
The things I seek, not love them less.

I love Love—though he has wings
   And like light can flee—
But above all other things,   45
   Spirit, I love thee—
Thou art Love and Life! O come,
Make once more my heart thy home.

An Exhortation

Written 1820. *Prometheus Unbound* (1820)

CHAMELEONS feed on light and air:
  Poets' food is love and fame:
If in this wide world of care
  Poets could but find the same
With as little toil as they,   5
    Would they ever change their hue
    As the light chameleons do,
      Suiting it to every ray
      Twenty times a day?

Poets are on this cold earth   10
  As chameleons might be,
Hidden from their early birth
  In a cave beneath the sea;
Where light is, chameleons change:
    Where love is not, Poets do: 15
    Fame is love disguised—if few
      Find either, never think it strange
      That Poets range.

Yet dare not stain with wealth or power
  A Poet's free and heavenly mind: 20
If bright chameleons should devour
  Any food but beams and wind
They would grow as earthly soon
    As their brother lizards are.—
    Children of a sunnier star,   25
      Spirits from beyond the moon,
      O, refuse the boon!

To a Skylark

Written June 1820. *Prometheus Unbound* (1820)

HAIL to thee, blithe Spirit!
  Bird thou never wert,
That from Heaven, or near it,
  Pourest thy full heart
In profuse strains of unpremeditated art.   5

Higher still and higher
  From the earth thou springest
Like a cloud of fire;
  The blue deep thou wingest,
And singing still dost soar, and soaring ever singest.   10

In the golden lightning
  Of the sunken Sun,
O'er which clouds are bright'ning,
  Thou dost float and run;
Like an unbodied joy whose race is just begun.   15

The pale purple even
  Melts around thy flight;
Like a star of Heaven
  In the broad daylight
Thou art unseen,—but yet I hear thy shrill delight,   20

Keen as are the arrows
  Of that silver sphere
Whose intense lamp narrows
  In the white dawn clear,
Until we hardly see—we feel that it is there.   25

All the earth and air
  With thy voice is loud,
As when night is bare
  From one lonely cloud
The moon rains out her beams, and Heaven is overflowed.   30

What thou art we know not;
  What is most like thee?
From rainbow clouds there flow nut
  Drops so bright to see
As from thy presence showers a rain of melody.   35

Like a Poet hidden
  In the light of thought,
Singing hymns unbidden
  Till the world is wrought
To sympathy with hopes and fears it heeded not: 40

Like a high-born maiden
  In a palace-tower,
Soothing her love-laden
  Soul in secret hour
With music sweet as love, which overflows her bower: 45

Like a glow-worm golden
  In a dell of dew,
Scattering unbeholden
  Its aërial hue
Among the flowers and grass which screen it from the
    view: 50

Like a rose embowered
  In its own green leaves,
By warm winds deflowered,
  Till the scent it gives

Makes faint with too much sweet those heavy-wingèd
  thieves: 55

   Sound of vernal showers
    On the twinkling grass,
   Rain-awakened flowers,
    All that ever was
Joyous and clear and fresh, thy music doth surpass.   60

   Teach us, Sprite or Bird,
    What sweet thoughts are thine;
   I have never heard
    Praise of love or wine
That panted forth a flood of rapture so divine: 65

   Chorus Hymeneal
    Or triumphal chant
   Matched with thine, would be all
    But an empty vaunt,
A thing wherein we feel there is some hidden want.   70

   What objects are the fountains
    Of thy happy strain,
   What fields or waves or mountains?
    What shapes of sky or plain?
What love of thine own kind? what ignorance of pain?   75

   With thy clear keen joyance
    Languor cannot be—
   Shadow of annoyance
    Never came near thee:
Thou lovest—but ne'er knew love's sad satiety.   80

Waking or asleep
Thou of death must deem
Things more true and deep
Than we mortals dream,
Or how could thy notes flow in such a crystal stream?   85

We look before and after,
And pine for what is not:
Our sincerest laughter
With some pain is fraught;
Our sweetest songs are those that tell of saddest thought.   90

Yet if we could scorn
Hate and pride and fear,
If we were things born
Not to shed a tear,
I know not how thy joy we ever should come near.   95

Better than all measures
Of delightful sound—
Better than all treasures
That in books are found—
Thy skill to poet were, thou scorner of the ground!   100

Teach me half the gladness
That thy brain must know,
Such harmonious madness
From my lips would flow
The world should listen then—as I am listening now.   105

The Cloud

Written 1820. *Prometheus Unbound* (1820)

I BRING fresh showers for the thirsting flowers,
  From the seas and the streams;
I bear light shade for the leaves when laid
  In their noonday dreams.
From my wings are shaken the dews that waken   5
  The sweet buds every one,
When rocked to rest on their mother's breast,
  As she dances about the sun.
I wield the flail of the lashing hail,
  And whiten the green plains under,   10
And then again I dissolve it in rain,
  And laugh as I pass in thunder.

I sift the snow on the mountains below,
  And their great pines groan aghast;
And all the night 'tis my pillow white,   15
  While I sleep in the arms of the blast.
Sublime on the towers of my skiey bowers,
  Lightning my pilot sits;
In a cavern under is fettered the thunder,
  It struggles and howls at fits;   20
Over earth and ocean, with gentle motion,
  This pilot is guiding me,
Lured by the love of the genii that move
  In the depths of the purple sea;
Over the rills, and the crags, and the hills,   25
  Over the lakes and the plains,
Wherever he dream, under mountain or stream
  The Spirit he loves remains;
And I all the while bask in heaven's blue smile,
  Whilst he is dissolving in rains.   30

The sanguine sunrise, with his meteor eyes,
    And his burning plumes outspread,
Leaps on the back of my sailing rack,
    When the morning star shines dead,
As on the jag of a mountain crag,   35
    Which an earthquake rocks and swings,
An eagle alit one moment may sit
    In the light of its golden wings.
And when sunset may breathe, from the lit sea beneath,
    Its ardours of rest and of love,   40
And the crimson pall of eve may fall
    From the depth of heaven above,
With wings folded I rest, on mine aery nest,
    As still as a brooding dove.

That orbèd maiden with white fire laden,   45
    Whom mortals call the moon,
Glides glimmering o'er my fleecelike floor
    By the midnight breezes strewn;
And wherever the beat of her unseen feet,
    Which only the angels hear,   50
May have broken the woof of my tent's thin roof,
    The stars peep behind her and peer;
And I laugh to see them whirl and flee,
    Like a swarm of golden bees,
When I widen the rent in my wind-built tent,   55
    Till the calm rivers, lakes, and seas,
Like strips of the sky fallen through me on high,
    Are each paved with the moon and these.

I bind the sun's throne with a burning zone,
    And the moon's with a girdle of pearl;   60
The volcanoes are dim, and the stars reel and swim,
    When the whirlwinds my banner unfurl.

From cape to cape, with a bridgelike shape,
 Over a torrent sea,
Sunbeam-proof, I hang like a roof,   65
 The mountains its columns be.
The triumphal arch through which I march
 With hurricane, fire, and snow,
When the Powers of the Air are chained to my chair,
 Is the million-coloured bow;   70
The sphere-fire above its soft colours wove,
 While the moist earth was laughing below.

I am the daughter of earth and water,
 And the nursling of the sky;
I pass through the pores of the oceans and shores;   75
 I change, but I cannot die—
For after the rain when with never a stain
 The pavilion of heaven is bare,
And the winds and sunbeams with their convex gleams
 Build up the blue dome of air,   80
I silently laugh at my own cenotaph,
 And out of the caverns of rain,
Like a child from the womb, like a ghost from the tomb,
 I arise, and unbuild it again.

Letter to the Gisbornes

Written 1–7 July 1820. Published 1824

THE spider spreads her webs whether she be
In poet's tower, cellar or barn or tree;
The silkworm in the dark green mulberry leaves
His winding sheet and cradle ever weaves;

So I, a thing whom moralists call worm,   5
Sit spinning still round this decaying form
From the fine threads of rare and subtle thought
—No net of words in garish colours wrought
To catch the idle buzzers of the day—
But a soft cell where, when that fades away,   10
Memory may clothe in wings my living name
And feed it with the asphodels of fame,
Which in those hearts that must remember me
Grow, making love an immortality.

Whoever should behold me now, I wist,   15
Would think I were a mighty mechanist
Bent with sublime Archimedean art
To breathe a soul into the iron heart
Of some machine portentous, or strange gin,
Which, by the force of figured spells, might win   20
Its way over the sea, and sport therein;
For round the walls are hung dread engines, such
As Vulcan never wrought for Jove to clutch
Ixion or the Titans;—or the quick
Wit of that man of God, St. Dominic,   25
To convince atheist, Turk or heretic;
Or those in philanthropic council met
Who thought to pay some interest for the debt
They owed to Jesus Christ for their salvation,
By giving a faint foretaste of damnation   30
To Shakespeare, Sidney, Spenser, and the rest
Who made our land an island of the blest,
When lamplike Spain, who now relumes her fire
On freedom's hearth, grew dim with empire—
With thumbscrews, wheels, with tooth and spike **and jag,** 35
Which fishers found under the utmost crag

Of Cornwall, and the storm-encompassed isles
Where to the sky the rude sea rarely smiles
Unless in treacherous wrath—as on the morn
When the exulting elements, in scorn,   40
Satiated with destroyed destruction, lay
Sleeping in beauty on their mangled prey
As panthers sleep.—And other strange and dread
Magical forms the brick floor overspread—
Proteus transformed to metal did not make   45
More figures or more strange, nor did he take
Such shapes of unintelligible brass,
Or heap himself in such a horrid mass
Of tin and iron not to be understood,
And forms of unimaginable wood,   50
To puzzle Tubal Cain and all his brood:
Great screws and cones and wheels and groovèd blocks,
The elements of what will stand the shocks
Of wave and wind and time.—Upon the table
More knacks and quips there be than I am able   55
To catalogize in this verse of mine—
A pretty bowl of wood, not full of wine
But quicksilver, that dew which the gnomes drink
When at their subterranean toil they swink,
Pledging the demons of the earthquake, who   60
Reply to them in lava, cry halloo!
And call out to the cities o'er their head
—Roofs, towers, and shrines, the dying and the dead,
Crash through the chinks of earth—and then all quaff
Another rouse, and hold their ribs and laugh.   65
This quicksilver no gnome has drunk—within
The walnut bowl it lies, veinèd and thin,
In colour like the wake of light that stains
The Tuscan deep, when from the moist moon rains

The inmost shower of its white fire—the breeze   70
Is still—blue heaven smiles over the pale seas;
And in this bowl of quicksilver—for I
Yield to the impulse of an infancy
Outlasting manhood—I have made to float
A rude idealism of a paper boat: 75
A hollow screw with cogs—Henry will know
The thing I mean, and laugh at me, if so
He fears not I should do more mischief—next
Lie bills and calculations much perplexed,
With steam boats, frigates and machinery quaint   80
Traced over them, in blue and yellow paint.
Then comes a range of mathematical
Instruments, for plans nautical and statical,
A heap of rosin, a queer broken glass
With ink in it, a china cup that was   85
What it will never be again, I think,
A thing from which sweet lips were wont to drink
The liquor doctors rail at, and which I
Will quaff in spite of them—and when we die
We'll toss up who died first of drinking tea,   90
And cry out heads or tails, where'er we be.
Near that a dusty paint box, some odd hooks,
A half-burnt match, an ivory block, three books
Where conic sections, spherics, logarithms,
To great Laplace from Saunderson and Sims   95
Lie heaped in their harmonious disarray
Of figures—disentangle them who may.
Baron de Tott's memoirs beside them lie,
And some odd volumes of old chemistry.
Near those a most inexplicable tin thing   100
With lead in the middle—I'm conjecturing

How to make Henry understand—but no,
I'll leave, as Spenser says, with many mo,
This secret in the pregnant womb of time,
Too vast a matter for so weak a rhyme.   105

And here like some weird Archimage sit I
Plotting dark spells and devilish enginery,
The self-impelling steam wheels of the mind
Which pump up oaths from clergymen, and grind
The gentle spirit of our meek reviews   110
Into a powdery foam of salt abuse,
Ruffling the dull wave of their self-content—
I sit and smile, or sigh, as is my bent,
But not for them—Libeccio rushes round
With an inconstant and an idle sound,   115
I heed him more than them—the thundersmoke
Is gathering on the mountains, like a cloak
Folded athwart their shoulders broad and bare;
The ripe corn under the undulating air
Undulates like an ocean, and the vines   120
Are trembling wide in all their trellised lines—
The murmur of the awakening sea doth fill
The empty pauses of the blast—the hill
Looks hoary through the white electric rain—
And from the glens beyond, in sullen strain   125
The interrupted thunder howls—above
One chasm of heaven smiles, like the eye of Love,
O'er the unquiet world—while such things are,
How could one worth your friendship heed this war
Of worms?—the shriek of the world's carrion jays,   130
Their censure, or their wonder, or their praise?

You are not here . . . the quaint witch Memory sees
In vacant chairs your absent images

And points where once you sat, and now should be
But are not—I demand if ever we   135
Shall meet as then we met—and she replies,
Veiling in awe her second-sighted eyes,
'I know the past alone—but summon home
My sister Hope—she speaks of all to come.'
But I, an old diviner, who know well   140
Every false verse of that sweet oracle,
Turned to the sad enchantress once again,
And sought a respite from my gentle pain
In citing every passage o'er and o'er
Of our communion—how on the sea shore   145
We watched the ocean and the sky together
Under the roof of blue Italian weather;
How I ran home through last year's thunderstorm,
And felt the transverse lightning linger warm
Upon my cheek—and how we often made   150
Feasts for each other, where good will outweighed
The frugal luxury of our country cheer,
As well it might, were it less firm and clear
Than ours must ever be—and how we spun
A shroud of talk to hide us from the sun   155
Of this familiar life which seems to be
But is not—or is but quaint mockery
Of all we would believe; or sadly blame
The jarring and inexplicable frame
Of this wrong world—and then anatomize   160
The purposes and thoughts of men whose eyes
Were closed in distant years—or widely guess
The issue of the earth's great business,
When we shall be, as we no longer are,
Like babbling gossips safe, who hear the war   165
Of winds, and sigh, but tremble not—or how

You listened to some interrupted flow
Of visionary rhyme, in joy and pain
Struck from the inmost fountains of my brain
With little skill perhaps—or how we sought   170
Those deepest wells of passion and of thought
Wrought by wise poets in the waste of years,
Staining their sacred waters with our tears,
Quenching a thirst ever to be renewed—
Or how I, wisest lady, then indued   175
The language of a land which now is free,
And winged with thoughts of truth and majesty
Flits round the tyrant's sceptre like a cloud,
And bursts the peopled prisons—cries aloud
'My name is Legion!', that majestic tongue   180
Which Calderon over the desert flung
Of ages and of nations, and which found
An echo in our hearts, and with the sound
Startled Oblivion—thou wert then to me
As is a nurse when inarticulately   185
A child would talk as its grown parents do.
If living winds the rapid clouds pursue,
If hawks chase doves through the etherial way,
Huntsmen the innocent deer, and beasts their prey,
Why should not we rouse with the spirit's blast   190
Out of the forest of the pathless past
These recollected pleasures?

                              You are now
In London, that great sea whose ebb and flow
At once is deaf and loud, and on the shore
Vomits its wrecks, and still howls on for more,   195
Yet in its depth what treasures! You will see
That which was Godwin,—greater none than he

Though fallen—and fallen on evil times—to stand
Among the spirits of our age and land,
Before the dread tribunal of *to come*   200
The foremost—while Rebuke cowers, pale and dumb.
You will see Coleridge, he who sits obscure
In the exceeding lustre and the pure
Intense irradiation of a mind
Which, with its own internal lightning blind,   205
Flags wearily through darkness and despair—
A cloud-encircled meteor of the air,
A hooded eagle among blinking owls.—
You will see Hunt, one of those happy souls
Who are the salt of the earth, and without whom   210
This world would smell like what it is, a tomb—
Who is, what others seem—his room, no doubt,
Is still adorned with many a cast from Shout,
With graceful flowers, tastefully placed about,
And coronals of bay from ribbons hung,   215
And brighter wreaths in neat disorder flung,
The gifts of the most learned among some dozens
Of female friends, sisters-in-law, and cousins,
And there is he with his eternal puns
Which beat the dullest brain for smiles, like duns   220
Thundering for money at a poet's door.
Alas, it is no use to say 'I'm poor!'
Or oft in graver mood, when he will look
Things wiser than were ever read in book,
Except in Shakespeare's wisest tenderness.   225
You will see Hogg—and I cannot express
His virtues, though I know that they are great,
Because he locks, then barricades the gate
Within which they inhabit—of his wit
And wisdom, you'll cry out when you are bit.   230

He is a pearl within an oyster shell,
One of the richest of the deep. And there
Is English Peacock with his mountain fair,
Turned into a Flamingo, that shy bird
That gleams i' the Indian air. Have you not heard   235
When a man marries, dies, or turns Hindoo,
His best friends hear no more of him? but you
Will see him and will like him too, I hope,
With the milk-white Snowdonian antelope
Matched with this cameleopard.—His fine wit   240
Makes such a wound, the knife is lost in it,
A strain too learnèd for a shallow age,
Too wise for selfish bigots—let his page
Which charms the chosen spirits of the time
Fold itself up for the serener clime   245
Of years to come, and find its recompense
In that just expectation.—Wit and sense,
Virtue, and human knowledge, all that might
Make this dull world a business of delight,
Are all combined in Horace Smith—and these,   250
With some exceptions which I need not tease
Your patience by descanting on, are all
You and I know in London—

                          I recall
My thoughts, and bid you look upon the night.
As water does a sponge, so the moonlight   255
Fills the void, hollow, universal air—
What see you? unpavilioned heaven is fair
Whether the moon, into her chamber gone,
Leaves midnight to the golden stars, or wan
Climbs with diminished beams the azure steep,   260
Or whether clouds sail o'er the inverse deep

Piloted by the many-wandering blast,
And the rare stars rush through them dim and fast—
All this is beautiful in every land—
But what see you beside?—a shabby stand   265
Of hackney coaches, a brick house or wall
Fencing some lordly court, white with the scrawl
Of our unhappy politics; or worse—
A wretched woman reeling by, whose curse
Mixed with the watchman's, partner of her trade,   270
You must accept in place of serenade—
Or yellow-haired Pollonia murmuring
To Henry some unutterable thing.—
I see a chaos of green leaves, and fruit
Built round dark caverns even to the root   275
Of the living stems which feed them—in whose bowers
There sleep in their dark dew the folded flowers;
Beyond, the surface of the unsickled corn
Trembles not in the slumbering air—and borne
In circles quaint, and ever-changing dance,   280
Like wingèd stars the fire-flies flash and glance
Pale in the open moonshine, but each one
Under the dark trees seems a little sun,
A meteor tamed, a fixed star gone astray
From the silver regions of the Milky Way;   285
Afar the contadino's song is heard,
Rude, but made sweet by distance—and a bird
Which cannot be the nightingale, and yet
I know none else that sings so sweet as it
At this late hour—and then all is still—   290
Now, Italy or London—which you will!

Next winter you must pass with me. I'll have
My house by that time turned into a grave

Of dead despondence and low-thoughted care
And all the dreams which our tormentors are.   295
Oh, that Hunt, Hogg, Peacock and Smith were there,
With everything belonging to them fair!
But we will have books, Spanish, Italian, Greek,
And ask one week to make another week
As like his father as I'm unlike mine,   300
Which is not his fault, as you may divine—
Though we eat little flesh and drink no wine
Yet let's be merry! we'll have tea and toast,
Custards for supper, and an endless host
Of syllabubs and jellies and mince-pies,   305
And other such lady-like luxuries—
Feasting on which, we will philosophize;
And we'll have fires out of the Grand Duke's wood
To thaw the six weeks' winter in our blood,
And then we'll talk—what shall we talk about?   310
Oh, there are themes enough for many a bout
Of thought-entangled descant;—as to nerves,
With cones and parallelograms and curves
I've sworn to strangle them if once they dare
To bother me—when you are with me there,   315
And they shall never more sip laudanum
From Helicon or Himeros;—well, come,
And in despite of God and of the devil
We'll make our friendly philosophic revel
Outlast the leafless time—till buds and flowers   320
Warn the obscure inevitable hours
Sweet meeting by sad parting to renew—
'Tomorrow to fresh woods and pastures new.'

The Pursued and the Pursuer

Written 1820. Published 1961

ARETHUSA was a maiden
  Bred among the rocks,
And Alpheus a shepherd, laden
    With the love of her sweet looks.
  More than all his flocks   5
    He loved those sweet looks.

A proud and an ungentle creature
  In her human form
Arethusa was by nature,
    And though fair and soft to see,   10
  Like a winter's storm
    To her love was she.

On a flattering fountain
  She would ever stare—
Till the maiden of the mountain   15
    Grew the thing she gazed upon,
  And mixed with waters there
    Fell from stone to stone.

Alpheus would weep and languish
  In a dell of dew,   20
Till his deep and liquid anguish
    Changed him to a gloomy river
  Whose dark waters must pursue
    Her bright waves, ever!

The pursued and the pursuer   25
    To the salt sea foam
Through the rocks and woods obscure
        Wound with murmur and with motion
    To the threshold of their home
        In the Dorian Ocean.   30

Apollo Sings
Written 1820. Published 1824

THE sleepless Hours who watch me as I lie
    Curtained with star-enwoven tapestries
From the broad moonlight of the open sky,
    Fanning the busy dreams from my dim eyes,—
Waken me when their mother, the grey Dawn,   5
Tells them that dreams and that the moon is gone.

Then I arise; and climbing Heaven's blue dome
    I walk over the mountains and the waves
Leaving my robe upon the ocean foam;
    My footsteps pave the clouds with fire; the caves   10
Are filled with my bright presence, and the air
Leaves the green Earth to my embraces bare.

The sunbeams are my shafts with which I kill
    Deceit, that loves the night and fears the day;
All men who do, or even imagine ill   15
    Fly me; and from the glory of my ray
Good minds and open actions take new might
Until diminished by the reign of night.

I feed the clouds, the rainbows and the flowers
    With their etherial colours; the moon's globe   20
And the pure stars in their eternal bowers
    Are cinctured with my power as with a robe;
Whatever lamps on Earth or Heaven may shine
Are portions of one spirit, which is mine.

I stand at noon upon the peak of Heaven;   25
    Then with unwilling steps, I linger down
Into the clouds of the Atlantic even;
    For grief that I depart they weep and frown—
What look is more delightful than the smile
With which I soothe them from the Western isle?   30

I am the eye with which the Universe
    Beholds itself, and knows it is divine;
All harmony of instrument and verse,
    All prophecy and medicine are mine,
All light of art or nature—to my song   35
Victory and praise, in its own right, belong.

Adonais

Written May–June 1821. *Adonais* (1821)

I

I WEEP for Adonais—he is dead!
O, weep for Adonais! though our tears
Thaw not the frost which binds so dear a head!
And thou, sad Hour, selected from all years
To mourn our loss, rouse thy obscure compeers,   5
And teach them thine own sorrow, say: with me
Died Adonais; till the Future dares
Forget the Past, his fate and fame shall be
An echo and a light unto eternity!

II

Where wert thou, mighty Mother, when he lay,   10
When thy Son lay, pierced by the shaft which flies
In darkness? where was lorn Urania
When Adonais died? With veilèd eyes,
'Mid listening Echoes, in her Paradise
She sat, while one, with soft enamoured breath,   15
Rekindled all the fading melodies
With which, like flowers that mock the corse beneath,
He had adorned and hid the coming bulk of death.

III

O, weep for Adonais—he is dead!
Wake, melancholy Mother, wake and weep!   20
Yet wherefore? Quench within their burning bed
Thy fiery tears, and let thy loud heart keep
Like his, a mute and uncomplaining sleep;
For he is gone, where all things wise and fair
Descend;—oh, dream not that the amorous Deep   25
Will yet restore him to the vital air;
Death feeds on his mute voice, and laughs at our despair.

IV

Most musical of mourners, weep again!
Lament anew, Urania!—He died,
Who was the Sire of an immortal strain,   30
Blind, old, and lonely, when his country's pride
The priest, the slave, and the liberticide
Trampled and mocked with many a loathèd rite
Of lust and blood; he went, unterrified,
Into the gulf of death; but his clear Sprite   35
Yet reigns o'er earth; the third among the sons of light.

V

Most musical of mourners, weep anew!
Not all to that bright station dared to climb;
And happier they their happiness who knew,
Whose tapers yet burn through that night of time   40
In which suns perished; others more sublime,
Struck by the envious wrath of man or God,
Have sunk, extinct in their refulgent prime;
And some yet live, treading the thorny road
Which leads, through toil and hate, to Fame's serene abode. 45

VI

But now, thy youngest, dearest one, has perished,
The nursling of thy widowhood, who grew,
Like a pale flower by some sad maiden cherished,
And fed with true love tears, instead of dew;
Most musical of mourners, weep anew!   50
Thy extreme hope, the loveliest and the last,
The bloom, whose petals nipped before they blew
Died on the promise of the fruit, is waste;
The broken lily lies—the storm is overpast.

VII

To that high Capital, where kingly Death   55
Keeps his pale court in beauty and decay,
He came; and bought, with price of purest breath,
A grave among the eternal.—Come away!
Haste, while the vault of blue Italian day
Is yet his fitting charnel-roof! while still   60
He lies, as if in dewy sleep he lay;
Awake him not! surely he takes his fill
Of deep and liquid rest, forgetful of all ill.

VIII

He will awake no more, oh, never more!—
Within the twilight chamber spreads apace   65
The shadow of white Death, and at the door
Invisible Corruption waits to trace
His extreme way to her dim dwelling-place;
The eternal Hunger sits, but pity and awe
Soothe her pale rage, nor dares she to deface   70
So fair a prey, till darkness, and the law
Of change, shall o'er his sleep the mortal curtain draw.

IX

O, weep for Adonais!—The quick Dreams,
The passion-wingèd Ministers of thought,
Who were his flocks, whom near the living streams   75
Of his young spirit he fed, and whom he taught
The love which was its music, wander not,—
Wander no more, from kindling brain to brain,
But droop there, whence they sprung; and mourn their lot
Round the cold heart, where, after their sweet pain,   80
They ne'er will gather strength, or find a home again.

X

And one with trembling hand clasps his cold head,
And fans him with her moonlight wings, and cries,
'Our love, our hope, our sorrow, is not dead;
See, on the silken fringe of his faint eyes,   85
Like dew upon a sleeping flower, there lies
A tear some Dream has loosened from his brain.'
Lost Angel of a ruined Paradise!
She knew not 'twas her own; as with no stain
She faded, like a cloud which had outwept its rain.   90

XI

One from a lucid urn of starry dew
Washed his light limbs as if embalming them;
Another clipped her profuse locks, and threw
The wreath upon him, like an anadem,
Which frozen tears instead of pearls begem;   95
Another in her wilful grief would break
Her bow and wingèd reeds, as if to stem
A greater loss with one which was more weak;
And dull the barbèd fire against his frozen cheek.

XII

Another Splendour on his mouth alit,   100
That mouth, whence it was wont to draw the breath
Which gave it strength to pierce the guarded wit,
And pass into the panting heart beneath
With lightning and with music: the damp death
Quenched its caress upon his icy lips;   105
And, as a dying meteor stains a wreath
Of moonlight vapour, which the cold night clips,
It flushed through his pale limbs, and passed to its eclipse.

XIII

And others came . . . Desires and Adorations,
Wingèd Persuasions and veiled Destinies,   110
Splendours, and Glooms, and glimmering Incarnations
Of hopes and fears, and twilight Phantasies;
And Sorrow, with her family of Sighs,
And Pleasure, blind with tears, led by the gleam
Of her own dying smile instead of eyes,   115
Came in slow pomp;—the moving pomp might seem
Like pageantry of mist on an autumnal stream.

XIV

All he had loved, and moulded into thought,
From shape, and hue, and odour, and sweet sound,
Lamented Adonais. Morning sought 120
Her eastern watch-tower, and her hair unbound,
Wet with the tears which should adorn the ground,
Dimmed the aërial eyes that kindle day;
Afar the melancholy thunder moaned,
Pale Ocean in unquiet slumber lay, 125
And the wild winds flew round, sobbing in their dismay.

XV

Lost Echo sits amid the voiceless mountains,
And feeds her grief with his remembered lay,
And will no more reply to winds or fountains,
Or amorous birds perched on the young green spray, 130
Or herdsman's horn, or bell at closing day,
Since she can mimic not his lips, more dear
Than those for whose disdain she pined away
Into a shadow of all sounds:—a drear
Murmur, between their songs, is all the woodmen hear. 135

XVI

Grief made the young Spring wild, and she threw down
Her kindling buds, as if she Autumn were,
Or they dead leaves; since her delight is flown,
For whom should she have waked the sullen year?
To Phoebus was not Hyacinth so dear 140
Nor to himself Narcissus, as to both
Thou, Adonais: wan they stand and sere
Amid the faint companions of their youth,
With dew all turned to tears; odour, to sighing ruth.

XVII

Thy spirit's sister, the lorn nightingale   145
Mourns not her mate with such melodious pain;
Not so the eagle, who like thee could scale
Heaven, and could nourish in the sun's domain
Her mighty youth with morning, doth complain,
Soaring and screaming round her empty nest,   150
As Albion wails for thee: the curse of Cain
Light on his head who pierced thy innocent breast,
And scared the angel soul that was its earthly guest!

XVIII

Ah, woe is me! Winter is come and gone,
But grief returns with the revolving year;   155
The airs and streams renew their joyous tone;
The ants, the bees, the swallows reappear;
Fresh leaves and flowers deck the dead Seasons' bier;
The amorous birds now pair in every brake,
And build their mossy homes in field and brere;   160
And the green lizard, and the golden snake,
Like unimprisoned flames, out of their trance awake.

XIX

Through wood and stream and field and hill and Ocean
A quickening life from the Earth's heart has burst
As it has ever done, with change and motion,   165
From the great morning of the world when first
God dawned on Chaos; in its stream immersed,
The lamps of Heaven flash with a softer light;
All baser things pant with life's sacred thirst;
Diffuse themselves; and spend in love's delight   170
The beauty and the joy of their renewèd might.

XX

The leprous corpse touched by this spirit tender
Exhales itself in flowers of gentle breath;
Like incarnations of the stars, when splendour
Is changed to fragrance, they illumine death   175
And mock the merry worm that wakes beneath;
Nought we know, dies. Shall that alone which knows
Be as a sword consumed before the sheath
By sightless lightning?—the intense atom glows
A moment, then is quenched in a most cold repose.   180

XXI

Alas! that all we loved of him should be,
But for our grief, as if it had not been,
And grief itself be mortal! Woe is me!
Whence are we, and why are we? of what scene
The actors or spectators? Great and mean   185
Meet massed in death, who lends what life must borrow.
As long as skies are blue, and fields are green,
Evening must usher night, night urge the morrow,
Month follow month with woe, and year wake year to sorrow.

XXII

He will awake no more, oh, never more!   190
'Wake thou,' cried Misery, 'childless Mother, rise
Out of thy sleep, and slake, in thy heart's core,
A wound more fierce than his with tears and sighs.'
And all the Dreams that watched Urania's eyes,
And all the Echoes whom their sister's song   195
Had held in holy silence, cried: 'Arise!'
Swift as a Thought by the snake Memory stung,
From her ambrosial rest the fading Splendour sprung.

XXIII

She rose like an autumnal Night, that springs
Out of the East, and follows wild and drear   200
The golden Day, which, on eternal wings,
Even as a ghost abandoning a bier,
Has left the Earth a corpse. Sorrow and fear
So struck, so roused, so rapt Urania;
So saddened round her like an atmosphere   205
Of stormy mist; so swept her on her way
Even to the mournful place where Adonais lay.

XXIV

Out of her secret Paradise she sped,
Through camps and cities rough with stone, and steel,
And human hearts, which to her aery tread   210
Yielding not, wounded the invisible
Palms of her tender feet where'er they fell:
And barbèd tongues, and thoughts more sharp than they,
Rent the soft Form they never could repel,
Whose sacred blood, like the young tears of May,   215
Paved with eternal flowers that undeserving way.

XXV

In the death chamber for a moment Death,
Shamed by the presence of that living Might,
Blushed to annihilation, and the breath
Revisited those lips, and life's pale light   220
Flashed through those limbs, so late her dear delight.
'Leave me not wild and drear and comfortless,
As silent lightning leaves the starless night!
Leave me not!' cried Urania: her distress
Roused Death: Death rose and smiled, and met her vain   225
    caress.

XXVI

'Stay yet awhile! speak to me once again;
Kiss me, so long but as a kiss may live;
And in my heartless breast and burning brain
That word, that kiss, shall all thoughts else survive,
With food of saddest memory kept alive,   230
Now thou art dead, as if it were a part
Of thee, my Adonais! I would give
All that I am to be as thou now art!
But I am chained to Time, and cannot thence depart!

XXVII

'Oh gentle child, beautiful as thou wert,   235
Why didst thou leave the trodden paths of men
Too soon, and with weak hands though mighty heart
Dare the unpastured dragon in his den?
Defenceless as thou wert, oh where was then
Wisdom the mirrored shield, or scorn the spear?   240
Or hadst thou waited the full cycle, when
Thy spirit should have filled its crescent sphere,
The monsters of life's waste had fled from thee like deer.

XXVIII

'The herded wolves, bold only to pursue;
The obscene ravens, clamorous o'er the dead;   245
The vultures to the conqueror's banner true
Who feed where Desolation first has fed,
And whose wings rain contagion;—how they fled,
When like Apollo, from his golden bow,
The Pythian of the age one arrow sped   250
And smiled!—The spoilers tempt no second blow,
They fawn on the proud feet that spurn them lying low.

XXIX

'The sun comes forth, and many reptiles spawn;
He sets, and each ephemeral insect then
Is gathered into death without a dawn,   255
And the immortal stars awake again;
So is it in the world of living men:
A godlike mind soars forth, in its delight
Making earth bare and veiling heaven, and when
It sinks, the swarms that dimmed or shared its light   260
Leave to its kindred lamps the spirit's awful night.'

XXX

Thus ceased she: and the mountain shepherds came,
Their garlands sere, their magic mantles rent;
The Pilgrim of Eternity, whose fame
Over his living head like Heaven is bent,   265
An early but enduring monument,
Came, veiling all the lightnings of his song
In sorrow; from her wilds Ierne sent
The sweetest lyrist of her saddest wrong,
And love taught grief to fall like music from his tongue. 270

XXXI

Midst others of less note, came one frail Form,
A phantom among men; companionless
As the last cloud of an expiring storm
Whose thunder is its knell; he, as I guess,
Had gazed on Nature's naked loveliness,   275
Actaeon-like, and now he fled astray
With feeble steps o'er the world's wilderness,
And his own thoughts, along that rugged way,
Pursued, like raging hounds, their father and their prey.

XXXII

A pardlike Spirit beautiful and swift—   280
A Love in desolation masked;—a Power
Girt round with weakness;—it can scarce uplift
The weight of the superincumbent hour;
It is a dying lamp, a falling shower,
A breaking billow;—even whilst we speak   285
Is it not broken? On the withering flower
The killing sun smiles brightly: on a cheek
The life can burn in blood, even while the heart may break.

XXXIII

His head was bound with pansies overblown,
And faded violets, white, and pied, and blue;   290
And a light spear topped with a cypress cone,
Round whose rude shaft dark ivy tresses grew
Yet dripping with the forest's noonday dew,
Vibrated, as the ever-beating heart
Shook the weak hand that grasped it; of that crew   295
He came the last, neglected and apart;
A herd-abandoned deer struck by the hunter's dart.

XXXIV

All stood aloof, and at his partial moan
Smiled through their tears; well knew that gentle band
Who in another's fate now wept his own—   300
As in the accents of an unknown land
He sang new sorrow; sad Urania scanned
The Stranger's mien, and murmured: 'Who art thou?'
He answered not, but with a sudden hand
Made bare his branded and ensanguined brow,   305
Which was like Cain's or Christ's—Oh! that it should be so!

XXXV

What softer voice is hushed over the dead?
Athwart what brow is that dark mantle thrown?
What form leans sadly o'er the white death-bed,
In mockery of monumental stone,   310
The heavy heart heaving without a moan?
If it be He, who, gentlest of the wise,
Taught, soothed, loved, honoured the departed one,
Let me not vex, with inharmonious sighs,
The silence of that heart's accepted sacrifice.   315

XXXVI

Our Adonais has drunk poison—oh!
What deaf and viperous murderer could crown
Life's early cup with such a draught of woe?
The nameless worm would now itself disown:
It felt, yet could escape, the magic tone   320
Whose prelude held all envy, hate, and wrong,
But what was howling in one breast alone,
Silent with expectation of the song,
Whose master's hand is cold, whose silver lyre unstrung.

XXXVII

Live thou, whose infamy is not thy fame!   325
Live! fear no heavier chastisement from me,
Thou noteless blot on a remembered name!
But be thyself, and know thyself to be!
And ever at thy season be thou free
To spill the venom when thy fangs o'erflow: 330
Remorse and Self-contempt shall cling to thee;
Hot Shame shall burn upon thy secret brow,
And like a beaten hound tremble thou shalt—as now.

XXXVIII

Nor let us weep that our delight is fled
Far from these carrion kites that scream below;   335
He wakes or sleeps with the enduring dead;
Thou canst not soar where he is sitting now.—
Dust to the dust! but the pure spirit shall flow
Back to the burning fountain whence it came,
A portion of the Eternal, which must glow   340
Through time and change, unquenchably the same,
Whilst thy cold embers choke the sordid hearth of shame.

XXXIX

Peace, peace! he is not dead, he doth not sleep—
He hath awakened from the dream of life—
'Tis we, who lost in stormy visions, keep   345
With phantoms an unprofitable strife,
And in mad trance, strike with our spirit's knife
Invulnerable nothings.—*We* decay
Like corpses in a charnel; fear and grief
Convulse us and consume us day by day,   350
And cold hopes swarm like worms within our living clay.

XL

He has outsoared the shadow of our night;
Envy and calumny and hate and pain,
And that unrest which men miscall delight,
Can touch him not and torture not again;   355
From the contagion of the world's slow stain
He is secure, and now can never mourn
A heart grown cold, a head grown grey in vain;
Nor, when the spirit's self has ceased to burn,
With sparkless ashes load an unlamented urn.   360

XLI

He lives, he wakes—'tis Death is dead, not he;
Mourn not for Adonais.—Thou young Dawn
Turn all thy dew to splendour, for from thee
The spirit thou lamentest is not gone;
Ye caverns and ye forests, cease to moan!   365
Cease ye faint flowers and fountains, and thou Air
Which like a mourning veil thy scarf hadst thrown
O'er the abandoned Earth, now leave it bare
Even to the joyous stars which smile on its despair!

XLII

He is made one with Nature: there is heard   370
His voice in all her music, from the moan
Of thunder, to the song of night's sweet bird;
He is a presence to be felt and known
In darkness and in light, from herb and stone,
Spreading itself where'er that Power may move   375
Which has withdrawn his being to its own;
Which wields the world with never wearied love,
Sustains it from beneath, and kindles it above.

XLIII

He is a portion of the loveliness
Which once he made more lovely: he doth bear   380
His part, while the one Spirit's plastic stress
Sweeps through the dull dense world, compelling there
All new successions to the forms they wear;
Torturing the unwilling dross that checks its flight
To its own likeness, as each mass may bear;   385
And bursting in its beauty and its might
From trees and beasts and men into the Heavens' light.

XLIV

The splendours of the firmament of time
May be eclipsed, but are extinguished not;
Like stars to their appointed height they climb 390
And death is a low mist which cannot blot
The brightness it may veil. When lofty thought
Lifts a young heart above its mortal lair,
And love and life contend in it, for what
Shall be its earthly doom, the dead live there 395
And move like winds of light on dark and stormy air.

XLV

The inheritors of unfulfilled renown
Rose from their thrones, built beyond mortal thought,
Far in the Unapparent. Chatterton
Rose pale, his solemn agony had not 400
Yet faded from him; Sidney, as he fought
And as he fell and as he lived and loved
Sublimely mild, a Spirit without spot,
Arose; and Lucan, by his death approved:
Oblivion as they rose shrank like a thing reproved. 405

XLVI

And many more, whose names on Earth are dark,
But whose transmitted effluence cannot die
So long as fire outlives the parent spark,
Rose, robed in dazzling immortality.
'Thou art become as one of us,' they cry, 410
'It was for thee yon kingless sphere has long
Swung blind in unascended majesty,
Silent alone amid an Heaven of song.
Assume thy wingèd throne, thou Vesper of our throng!'

XLVII

Who mourns for Adonais? oh, come forth   415
Fond wretch! and know thyself and him aright.
Clasp with thy panting soul the pendulous Earth;
As from a centre, dart thy spirit's light
Beyond all worlds, until its spacious might
Satiate the void circumference: then shrink   420
Even to a point within our day and night;
And keep thy heart light lest it make thee sink
When hope has kindled hope, and lured thee to the brink;

XLVIII

Or go to Rome, which is the sepulchre,
O, not of him, but of our joy: 'tis nought   425
That ages, empires, and religions there
Lie buried in the ravage they have wrought;
For such as he can lend,—they borrow not
Glory from those who made the world their prey;
And he is gathered to the kings of thought   430
Who waged contention with their time's decay,
And of the past are all that cannot pass away.

XLIX

Go thou to Rome,—at once the Paradise,
The grave, the city, and the wilderness;
And where its wrecks like shattered mountains rise,   435
And flowering weeds, and fragrant copses dress
The bones of Desolation's nakedness
Pass, till the Spirit of the spot shall lead
Thy footsteps to a slope of green access
Where, like an infant's smile, over the dead,   440
A light of laughing flowers along the grass is spread.

L

And gray walls moulder round, on which dull Time
Feeds, like slow fire upon a hoary brand;
And one keen pyramid with wedge sublime,
Pavilioning the dust of him who planned   445
This refuge for his memory, doth stand
Like flame transformed to marble; and beneath,
A field is spread, on which a newer band
Have pitched in Heaven's smile their camp of death,
Welcoming him we lose with scarce extinguished breath.   450

LI

Here pause: these graves are all too young as yet
To have outgrown the sorrow which consigned
Its charge to each; and if the seal is set,
Here, on one fountain of a mourning mind,
Break it not thou! too surely shalt thou find   455
Thine own well full, if thou returnest home,
Of tears and gall. From the world's bitter wind
Seek shelter in the shadow of the tomb.
What Adonais is, why fear we to become?

LII

The One remains, the many change and pass;   460
Heaven's light forever shines, Earth's shadows fly;
Life, like a dome of many-coloured glass,
Stains the white radiance of Eternity,
Until Death tramples it to fragments.—Die,
If thou wouldst be with that which thou dost seek!   465
Follow where all is fled!—Rome's azure sky,
Flowers, ruins, statues, music, words, are weak
The glory they transfuse with fitting truth to speak.

LIII

Why linger, why turn back, why shrink, my Heart?
Thy hopes are gone before: from all things here   470
They have departed; thou shouldst now depart!
A light is passed from the revolving year,
And man, and woman; and what still is dear
Attracts to crush, repels to make thee wither.
The soft sky smiles,—the low wind whispers near: 475
'Tis Adonais calls! oh, hasten thither,
No more let Life divide what Death can join together.

LIV

That Light whose smile kindles the Universe,
That Beauty in which all things work and move,
That Benediction which the eclipsing Curse   480
Of birth can quench not, that sustaining Love
Which through the web of being blindly wove
By man and beast and earth and air and sea,
Burns bright or dim, as each are mirrors of
The fire for which all thirst, now beams on me,   485
Consuming the last clouds of cold mortality.

LV

The breath whose might I have invoked in song
Descends on me; my spirit's bark is driven
Far from the shore, far from the trembling throng
Whose sails were never to the tempest given;   490
The massy earth and spherèd skies are riven!
I am borne darkly, fearfully, afar;
Whilst burning through the inmost veil of Heaven,
The soul of Adonais, like a star,
Beacons from the abode where the Eternal are.   495

The Aziola

Written 1821. Published 1829

'Do you not hear the aziola cry?
Methinks she must be nigh—'
    Said Mary as we sat
In dusk, ere stars were lit or candles brought—
    And I who thought   5
This Aziola was some tedious woman
Asked, 'Who is Aziola?'—how elate
I felt to know that it was nothing human,
No mockery of myself to fear or hate!
    And Mary saw my soul   10
And laughed, and said—'Disquiet yourself not,
    'Tis nothing but a little downy owl.'

Sad aziola, many an eventide
    Thy music I had heard
By wood and stream, meadow and mountainside,   15
And fields and marshes wide,
Such as nor voice, nor lute, nor wind, nor bird
    The soul ever stirred—
Unlike and far sweeter than them all.
Sad aziola, from that moment I   20
Loved thee and thy sad cry.

Two Choruses of Greek Captive Women, from *Hellas*

Written autumn 1821. *Hellas* (1822)

I

WORLDS on worlds are rolling ever
  From creation to decay,
Like the bubbles on a river
  Sparkling, bursting, borne away.
    But they are still immortal   5
    Who through birth's orient portal
And death's dark chasm hurrying to and fro,
    Clothe their unceasing flight
    In the brief dust and light
Gathered around their chariots as they go;   10
    New shapes they still may weave,
    New gods, new laws receive,
Bright or dim are they as the robes they last
    On Death's bare ribs had cast.

A Power from the unknown God,   15
  A Promethean conqueror, came;
Like a triumphal path he trod
  The thorns of death and shame.
    A mortal shape to him
    Was like the vapour dim   20
Which the orient planet animates with light;
    Hell, Sin, and Slavery came
    Like bloodhounds mild and tame,
Nor preyed, until their Lord had taken flight;

The moon of Mahomet   25
Arose, and it shall set
While blazoned as on Heaven's immortal noon
The cross leads generations on.

Swift as the radiant shapes of sleep
From one whose dreams are Paradise   30
Fly, when the fond wretch wakes to weep
And Day peers forth with her blank eyes,
So fleet, so faint, so fair
The Powers of earth and air
Fled from the folding-star of Bethlehem: 35
Apollo, Pan, and Love,
And even Olympian Jove
Grew weak, for killing Truth had glared on them;
Our hills and seas and streams
Dispeopled of their dreams,   40
Their waters turned to blood, their dew to tears,
Wailed for the golden years.

II

The world's great age begins anew,
The golden years return,
The earth doth like a snake renew
Her winter weeds outworn;
Heaven smiles, and faiths and empires gleam   5
Like wrecks of a dissolving dream.

A brighter Hellas rears its mountains
From waves serener far,
A new Peneus rolls his fountains
Against the morning-star;   10
Where fairer Tempes bloom, there sleep
Young Cyclads on a sunnier deep.

A loftier Argo cleaves the main
   Fraught with a later prize;
Another Orpheus sings again,   15
   And loves, and weeps, and dies;
A new Ulysses leaves once more
Calypso for his native shore.

O, write no more the tale of Troy
   If earth Death's scroll must be!   20
Nor mix with Laian rage the joy
   Which dawns upon the free;
Although a subtler Sphinx renew
Riddles of death Thebes never knew.

Another Athens shall arise   25
   And to remoter time
Bequeath, like sunset to the skies,
   The splendour of its prime,
And leave, if nought so bright may live,
All earth can take or Heaven can give.   30

Saturn and Love their long repose
   Shall burst, more bright and good
Than all who fell, than One who rose,
   Than many unsubdued;
Not gold, not blood, their altar dowers,   35
But votive tears and symbol flowers.

O cease! must hate and death return?
   Cease! must men kill and die?
Cease! drain not to its dregs the urn
   Of bitter prophecy.   40
The world is weary of the past,
O might it die or rest at last!

To Jane. The Invitation

Written spring 1822. Published 1839

BEST and brightest, come away—
Fairer far than this fair day
Which, like thee to those in sorrow,
Comes to bid a sweet good-morrow
To the rough year just awake   5
In its cradle on the brake.
The brightest hour of unborn spring
Through the winter wandering
Found, it seems, this halcyon morn
To hoar February born;   10
Bending from Heaven in azure mirth
It kissed the forehead of the earth,
And smiled upon the silent sea,
And bade the frozen streams be free
And waked to music all their fountains,   15
And breathed upon the frozen mountains,
And like a prophetess of May
Strewed flowers upon the barren way,
Making the wintry world appear
Like one on whom thou smilest, dear.   20

Away, away from men and towns
To the wild wood and the downs,
To the silent wilderness
Where the soul need not repress
Its music lest it should not find   25
An echo in another's mind,
While the touch of Nature's art
Harmonizes heart to heart.

I leave this notice on my door
For each accustomed visitor—   30
'I am gone into the fields
To take what this sweet hour yields.
Reflection, you may come tomorrow,
Sit by the fireside with Sorrow—
You, with the unpaid bill, Despair;   35
You, tiresome verse-reciter, Care,
I will pay you in the grave,
Death will listen to your stave—
Expectation too, be off!
Today is for itself enough—   40
Hope, in pity mock not woe
With smiles, nor follow where I go;
Long having lived on thy sweet food,
At length I find one moment's good
After long pain—with all your love   45
This you never told me of.'

Radiant Sister of the day,
Awake, arise and come away
To the wild woods and the plains,
And the pools where winter-rains   50
Image all their roof of leaves,
Where the pine its garland weaves
Of sapless green and ivy dun
Round stems that never kiss the Sun—
Where the lawns and pastures be,   55
And the sandhills of the sea—
When the melting hoar-frost wets
The daisy-star that never sets;
And wind-flowers, and violets

Which yet join not scent to hue,   60
Crown the pale year weak and new;
When the night is left behind
In the deep east dun and blind,
And the blue noon is over us,
And the multitudinous   65
Billows murmur at our feet
Where the earth and ocean meet,
And all things seem only one
In the universal Sun.

From The Triumph of Life

Written May–June 1822, unfinished. Published 1824

SWIFT as a spirit hastening to his task
  Of glory and of good, the Sun sprang forth
Rejoicing in his splendour, and the mask

  Of darkness fell from the awakened Earth.
The smokeless altars of the mountain snows   5
  Flamed above crimson clouds, and at the birth

Of light the ocean's orison arose
  To which the birds tempered their matin lay.
All flowers in field or forest which unclose

  Their trembling eyelids to the kiss of day,   10
Swinging their censers in the element,
  With orient incense lit by the new ray

Burned slow and inconsumably, and sent
  Their odorous sighs up to the smiling air,
And in succession due, did continent,   15

Isle, ocean, and all things that in them wear
The form and character of mortal mould
    Rise as the Sun their father rose, to bear

Their portion of the toil which he of old
    Took as his own and then imposed on them;   20
But I, whom thoughts which must remain untold

    Had kept as wakeful as the stars that gem
The cone of night, now they were laid asleep,
    Stretched my faint limbs beneath the hoary stem

Which an old chestnut flung athwart the steep   25
    Of a green Apennine: before me fled
The night; behind me rose the day; the deep

    Was at my feet, and heaven above my head;
When a strange trance over my fancy grew
    Which was not slumber, for the shade it spread   30

Was so transparent that the scene came through
    As clear as when a veil of light is drawn
O'er evening hills they glimmer; and I knew

    That I had felt the freshness of that dawn,
Bathed in the same cold dew my brow and hair,   35
    And sat as thus upon that slope of lawn

Under the self-same bough, and heard as there
    The birds, the fountains, and the ocean hold
Sweet talk in music through the enamoured air.
    And then a Vision on my brain was rolled . . .   40

As in that trance of wondrous thought I lay
  This was the tenour of my waking dream:
Methought I sat beside a public way

  Thick strewn with summer dust, and a great stream
Of people there was hurrying to and fro 45
  Numerous as gnats upon the evening gleam,

All hastening onward, yet none seemed to know
  Whither he went, or whence he came, or why
He made one of the multitude, yet so

  Was borne amid the crowd as through the sky 50
One of the million leaves of summer's bier:
  Old age and youth, manhood and infancy,

Mixed in one mighty torrent did appear,
  Some flying from the thing they feared, and some
Seeking the object of another's fear, 55

  And others as with steps towards the tomb
Pored on the trodden worms that crawled beneath,
  And others mournfully within the gloom

Of their own shadow walked, and called it death . . .
  And some fled from it as it were a ghost, 60
Half fainting in the affliction of vain breath;

  But more, with motions which each other crossed,
Pursued or shunned the shadows the clouds threw
  Or birds within the noonday ether lost,

Upon that path where flowers never grew,　　65
　　And weary with vain toil and faint for thirst
Heard not the fountains whose melodious dew

　　Out of their mossy cells forever burst,
Nor felt the breeze which from the forest told
　　Of grassy paths, and wood-lawns interspersed　　70

With overarching elms, and caverns cold,
　　And violet banks where sweet dreams brood, but they
Pursued their serious folly as of old . . .

　　And as I gazed methought that in the way
The throng grew wilder, as the woods of June　　75
　　When the south wind shakes the extinguished day,

And a cold glare, intenser than the noon,
　　But icy cold, obscured with [　　　] light
The sun, as he the stars. Like the young moon

　　When on the sunlit limits of the night　　80
Her white shell trembles amid crimson air
　　And whilst the sleeping tempest gathers might

Doth, as a herald of its coming, bear
　　The ghost of her dead mother, whose dim form
Bends in dark ether from her infant's chair,　　85

　　So came a chariot on the silent storm
Of its own rushing splendour, and a Shape
　　So sat within as one whom years deform

Beneath a dusky hood and double cape
　　Crouching within the shadow of a tomb,　　90
And o'er what seemed the head a cloud, like crape,

Was bent, a dun and faint etherial gloom
Tempering the light; upon the chariot's beam
  A Janus-visaged Shadow did assume

The guidance of that wonder-wingèd team.   95
  The shapes which drew it in thick lightnings
Were lost: I heard alone on the air's soft stream

  The music of their ever-moving wings.
All the four faces of that charioteer
  Had their eyes banded . . . little profit brings   100

Speed in the van and blindness in the rear,
  Nor then avail the beams that quench the Sun,
Or that their banded eyes could pierce the sphere

  Of all that is, has been, or will be done,
So ill was the car guided; but it passed   105
  With solemn speed majestically on . . .

The crowd gave way, and I arose aghast,
  Or seemed to rise, so mighty was the trance,
And saw like clouds upon the thunder-blast

  The million with fierce song and maniac dance   110
Raging around: such seemed the jubilee
  As when to greet some conqueror's advance

Imperial Rome poured forth her living sea
  From senate-house and prison and theatre,
When [   ] upon the free   115

  Had bound a yoke which soon they stooped to bear.
Nor wanted here the just similitude
  Of a triumphal pageant, for where'er

The chariot rolled, a captive multitude
  Was driven: all those who had grown old in power   120
Or misery,—all who have their age subdued

  By action or by suffering, and whose hour
Was drained to its last sand in weal or woe,
  So that the trunk survived both fruit and flower;

All those whose fame or infamy must grow   125
  Till the great winter lay the form and name
Of their fair earth with them forever low,

—All but the sacred few who could not tame
Their spirits to the Conqueror, but as soon
  As they had touched the world with living flame   130

Fled back like eagles to their native noon,
  Or those who put aside the diadem
Of earthly thrones or gems—till the last one

  Were there: for they of Athens and Jerusalem
Were neither mid the mighty captives seen,   135
  Nor mid the ribald crowd that followed them,

Nor those who went before . . . Fierce and obscene
  The wild dance maddens in the van, and those
Who lead it, fleet as shadows on the green,

  Outspeed the chariot and without repose   140
Mix with each other in tempestuous measure
  To savage music. . . Wilder as it grows,

They, tortured by their agonizing pleasure,
  Convulsed, and on the rapid whirlwinds spun
Of that fierce Spirit whose unholy leisure   145

Was soothed by mischief since the world begun,
Throw back their heads and loose their streaming hair,
    And in their dance round her who dims the Sun

Maidens and youths fling their wild arms in air
    As their feet twinkle; now they recede, and now,   150
Bending within each other's atmosphere

    Kindle invisibly; and as they glow
Like moths by light attracted and repelled,
    Oft to their bright destruction come and go,

Till—like two clouds into one vale impelled   155
    That shake the mountains when their lightnings mingle,
And die in rain—the fiery band which held

    Their natures, snaps . . . while the shocks still may tingle
One falls and then another in the path
    Senseless, nor is the desolation single,   160

Yet ere I can say *where*, the chariot hath
    Passed over them; nor other trace I find
But as of foam after the ocean's wrath

    Is spent upon the desert shore.—Behind,
Old men and women foully disarrayed   165
    Shake their grey hair in the insulting wind,

Grasp in the dance and strain with limbs decayed
    To reach the car of light which leaves them still
Far behind, and deeper in the shade.

    But not the less with impotence of will   170
They wheel, though ghastly shadows interpose,
    Round them and round each other, and fulfil

Their work, and to the dust whence they arose
  Sink, and corruption veils them as they lie,
And frost in these performs what fire in those.   175

  Struck to the heart by this sad pageantry,
Half to myself I said, 'And what is this?
  Whose shape is that within the car? and why—'

I would have added—'is all here amiss?'
  But a voice answered: 'Life' . . . I turned and knew   180
(O Heaven have mercy on such wretchedness!)

  That what I thought was an old root which grew
To strange distortion out of the hill side
  Was indeed one of that deluded crew,

And that the grass which methought hung so wide   185
  And white, was but his thin discoloured hair,
And that the holes it vainly sought to hide

  Were, or had been, eyes.—'If thou canst forbear
To join the dance, which I had well forborne,'
  Said the grim Feature, of my thought aware,   190

'I will tell all that which to this deep scorn
  Led me and my companions, and relate
The progress of the pageant since the morn;

  'If thirst of knowledge shall not thus abate,
Follow it thou even to the night, but I   195
  Am weary' . . . then like one who with the weight

Of his own words is staggered, wearily
  He paused, and ere he could resume, I cried:
'First, who art thou?' . . . 'Before thy memory

'I feared, loved, hated, suffered, did, and died,   200
And if the spark with which Heaven lit my spirit
  Earth had with purer nutriment supplied

'Corruption would not now thus much inherit
  Of what was once Rousseau—nor this disguise
Stain that which ought to have disdained to wear it;   205

  'If I have been extinguished, yet there rise
A thousand beacons from the spark I bore.'
  'And who are those chained to the car?' 'The wise,

'The great, the unforgotten: they who wore
  Mitres and helms and crowns, or wreaths of light   210
Signs of thought's empire over thought; their lore

  'Taught them not this—to know themselves; their might
Could not repress the mutiny within,
  And for the morn of truth they feigned, deep night

'Caught them ere evening.'   215

Lines written in the Bay of Lerici

Written late June, 1822. Published 1862

BRIGHT wanderer, fair coquette of Heaven,
To whom alone it has been given
To change and be adored for ever,
Envy not this dim world, for never
But once within its shadow grew   5
One fair as you, but far more true.
She left me at the silent time
When the moon had ceased to climb

The azure dome of Heaven's steep,
And like an albatross asleep,   10
Balanced on her wings of light
Hovered in the purple night,
Ere she sought her Ocean nest
In the chambers of the west.—
She left me, and I stayed alone   15
Thinking over every tone,
Which though now silent to the ear
The enchanted heart could hear
Like notes which die when born, but still
Haunt the echoes of the hill: 20
And feeling ever—o, too much—
The soft vibrations of her touch
As if her gentle hand even now
Lightly trembled on my brow;
And thus although she absent were   25
Memory gave me all of her
That even fancy dares to claim.—
Her presence had made weak and tame
All passions, and I lived alone
In the time which is our own;   30
The past and future were forgot,
As they had been, and would be, not.—
But soon, the guardian angel gone,
The demon reassumed his throne
In my faint heart . . . I dare not speak   35
My thoughts; but thus disturbed and weak
I sat and watched the vessels glide
Along the Ocean bright and wide,
Like spirit-wingèd chariots sent
O'er some serenest element   40

For ministrations strange and far;
As if to some Elysian star
They sailed for drink to medicine
Such sweet and bitter pain as mine.—
And the wind that winged their flight   45
From the land came fresh and light,
And the scent of sleeping flowers
And the coolness of the hours
Of dew, and the sweet warmth of day
Was scattered o'er the twinkling bay;   50
And the fisher with his lamp
And spear, about the low rocks damp
Crept, and struck the fish who came
To worship the delusive flame:
Too happy, they whose pleasure sought   55
Extinguishes all sense and thought
Of the regret that pleasure [   ]
Seeking Life alone *not peace*.

PROSE

From A Defence of Poetry

POETRY, in a general sense, may be defined to be 'the expression of the imagination:' and poetry is connate with the origin of man. Man is an instrument over which a series of external and internal impressions are driven, like the alternations of an ever-changing wind over an Æolian 5 lyre, which move it by their motion to ever-changing melody. But there is a principle within the human being, and perhaps within all sentient beings, which acts other-wise than in a lyre, and produces not melody alone, but harmony, by an internal adjustment of the sounds and 10 motions thus excited to the impressions which excite them. It is as if the lyre could accommodate its chords to the motions of that which strikes them, in a determined pro-portion of sound; even as the musician can accommodate his voice to the sound of the lyre. . . . 15

In the youth of the world, men dance and sing and imitate natural objects, observing in these actions, as in all others, a certain rhythm or order. And, although all men observe a similar, they observe not the same order, in the motions of the dance, in the melody of the song, in the 20 combinations of language, in the series of their imitations of natural objects. For there is a certain order or rhythm belonging to each of these classes of mimetic representa-tion, from which the hearer and the spectator receive an intenser and purer pleasure than from any other: the 25 sense of an approximation to this order has been called taste by modern writers. Every man in the infancy of art, observes an order which approximates more or less closely to that from which this highest delight results: but the diversity is not sufficiently marked, as that its gradations should be sensible, except in those instances where the predominance of this faculty of approximation to the beautiful (for so we may be permitted to name the relation between this highest pleasure and its cause) is very great. Those in whom it exists to excess are poets, in the most universal sense of the word; and the pleasure resulting from the manner in which they express the influence of society or nature upon their own minds, communicates itself to others, and gathers a sort of reduplication from the community. Their language is vitally metaphorical; that is, it marks the before unapprehended relations of things and perpetuates their apprehension, until words, which represent them, become, through time, signs for portions or classes of thought, instead of pictures of integral thoughts; and then, if no new poets should arise to create afresh the associations which have been thus disorganized, language will be dead to all the nobler purposes of human intercourse. . . .

But poets, or those who imagine and express this indestructible order, are not only the authors of language and of music, of the dance, and architecture, and statuary, and painting; they are the institutors of laws and the founders of civil society, and the inventors of the arts of life, and the teachers, who draw into a certain propinquity with the beautiful and the true, that partial apprehension of the agencies of the invisible world which is called religion. Hence all original religions are allegorical or susceptible of allegory, and, like Janus, have a double face of false and true. Poets, according to the

circumstances of the age and nation in which they appeared, 60
were called, in the earlier epochs of the world, legislators
or prophets: a poet essentially comprises and unites both
these characters. For he not only beholds intensely the
present as it is, and discovers those laws according to which
present things ought to be ordered, but he beholds the 65
future in the present, and his thoughts are the germs of
the flower and the fruit of latest time. Not that I assert
poets to be prophets in the gross sense of the word, or that
they can foretell the form as surely as they foreknow
the spirit of events: such is the pretence of superstition, 70
which would make poetry an attribute of prophecy, rather
than prophecy an attribute of poetry. A poet participates
in the eternal, the infinite, and the one; as far as relates to
his conceptions, time and place and number are not. . . .
But poetry in a more restricted sense expresses those 75
arrangements of language, and especially metrical language, which are created by that imperial faculty, whose
throne is curtained within the invisible nature of man.
And this springs from the nature itself of language,
which is a more direct representation of the actions and 80
passions of our internal being, and is susceptible of more
various and delicate combinations, than colour, form, or
motion, and is more plastic and obedient to the control of
that faculty of which it is the creation. For language is
arbitrarily produced by the imagination, and has relation 85
to thoughts alone; but all other materials, instruments,
and conditions of art, have relations among each other,
which limit and interpose between conception and expression. The former is as a mirror which reflects, the latter
as a cloud which enfeebles, the light of which both are 90
mediums of communication. . . .

The distinction between poets and prose writers is a

vulgar error. . . . All the authors of revolutions in opinion
are not only necessarily poets as they are inventors, nor
even as their words unveil the permanent analogy of 95
things by images which participate in the life of truth; but
as their periods are harmonious and rhythmical, and
contain in themselves the elements of verse; being the
echo of the eternal music. Nor are those supreme poets,
who have employed traditional forms of rhythm on 100
account of the form and action of their subjects, less
capable of perceiving and teaching the truth of things,
than those who have omitted that form. Shakespeare,
Dante, and Milton (to confine ourselves to modern
writers) are philosophers of the very loftiest power.   105

A poem is the very image of life expressed in its eternal
truth. There is this difference between a story and a poem,
that a story is a catalogue of detached facts, which have
no other connexion than time, place, circumstance, cause,
and effect; the other is the creation of actions according 110
to the unchangeable forms of human nature, as existing in
the mind of the Creator, which is itself the image of all
other minds. The one is partial, and applies only to a
definite period of time, and a certain combination of events
which can never again recur; the other is universal, and 115
contains within itself the germ of a relation to whatever
motives or actions have place in the possible varieties of
human nature. Time, which destroys the beauty and the
use of the story of particular facts, stripped of the poetry
which should invest them, augments that of poetry, and 120
for ever develops new and wonderful applications of the
eternal truth which it contains. Hence epitomes have
been called the moths of just history; they eat out the
poetry of it. A story of particular facts is as a mirror which
obscures and distorts that which should be beautiful: 125

poetry is a mirror which makes beautiful that which is distorted. . . .

Having determined what is poetry, and who are poets, let us proceed to estimate its effects upon society.

Poetry is ever accompanied with pleasure: all spirits 130 upon which it falls open themselves to receive the wisdom which is mingled with its delight. In the infancy of the world, neither poets themselves nor their auditors are fully aware of the excellence of poetry: for it acts in a divine and unapprehended manner, beyond and above conscious- 135 ness; and it is reserved for future generations to contemplate and measure the mighty cause and effect in all the strength and splendour of their union. Even in modern times, no living poet ever arrived at the fullness of his fame; the jury which sits in judgment upon a poet, 140 belonging as he does to all time, must be composed of his peers: it must be empanelled by time from the selectest of the wise of many generations. A poet is a nightingale, who sits in darkness and sings to cheer its own solitude with sweet sounds; his auditors are as men entranced by the 145 melody of an unseen musician, who feel that they are moved and softened, yet know not whence or why. The poems of Homer and his contemporaries were the delight of infant Greece; they were the elements of that social system which is the column upon which all succeeding 150 civilization has reposed. Homer embodied the ideal perfection of his age in human character; nor can we doubt that those who read his verses were awakened to an ambition of becoming like to Achilles, Hector, and Ulysses: the truth and beauty of friendship, patriotism, 155 and persevering devotion to an object, were unveiled to their depths in these immortal creations: the sentiments of the auditors must have been refined and enlarged by a

sympathy with such great and lovely impersonations, until
from admiring they imitated, and from imitation they 160
identified themselves with the objects of their admiration.
Nor let it be objected, that these characters are remote
from moral perfection, and that they are by no means to
be considered as edifying patterns for general imitation.
Every epoch, under names more or less specious, has 165
deified its peculiar errors; Revenge is the naked idol of the
worship of a semibarbarous age; and Self-deceit is the
veiled image of unknown evil, before which luxury and
satiety lie prostrate. But a poet considers the vices of his
contemporaries as the temporary dress in which his 170
creations must be arrayed, and which cover without
concealing the eternal proportions of their beauty. An
epic or dramatic personage is understood to wear them
around his soul, as he may the ancient armour or modern
uniform around his body; whilst it is easy to conceive a 175
dress more graceful than either. The beauty of the internal
nature cannot be so far concealed by its accidental vesture,
but that the spirit of its form shall communicate itself to
the very disguise, and indicate the shape it hides from the
manner in which it is worn. A majestic form and graceful 180
motions will express themselves through the most bar-
barous and tasteless costume. Few poets of the highest
class have chosen to exhibit the beauty of their conceptions in its naked truth and splendour; and it is doubtful
whether the alloy of costume, habit, etc., be not necessary 185
to temper this planetary music for mortal ears.

The whole objection, however, of the immorality of
poetry rests upon a misconception of the manner in which
poetry acts to produce the moral improvement of man.
Ethical science arranges the elements which poetry has 190
created, and propounds schemes and proposes examples

of civil and domestic life: nor is it for want of admirable
doctrines that men hate, and despise, and censure, and
deceive, and subjugate one another. But poetry acts in
another and diviner manner. It awakens and enlarges the 195
mind itself by rendering it the receptacle of a thousand
unapprehended combinations of thought. Poetry lifts the
veil from the hidden beauty of the world, and makes
familiar objects be as if they were not familiar; it reproduces all that it represents, and the impersonations clothed 200
in its Elysian light stand thenceforward in the minds of
those who have once contemplated them, as memorials of
that gentle and exalted content which extends itself over
all thoughts and actions with which it coexists. The great
secret of morals is love; or a going out of our own nature, 205
and an identification of ourselves with the beautiful which
exists in thought, action, or person, not our own. A man,
to be greatly good, must imagine intensely and compre-
hensively; he must put himself in the place of another and
of many others; the pains and pleasures of his species must 210
become his own. The great instrument of moral good is
the imagination; and poetry administers to the effect by
acting upon the cause. Poetry enlarges the circumference
of the imagination by replenishing it with thoughts of ever
new delight, which have the power of attracting and 215
assimilating to their own nature all other thoughts, and
which form new intervals and interstices whose void for
ever craves fresh food. Poetry strengthens the faculty
which is the organ of the moral nature of man, in the same
manner as exercise strengthens a limb. A poet therefore 220
would do ill to embody his own conceptions of right and
wrong, which are usually those of his place and time, in
his poetical creations, which participate in neither. . . .

The poetry of Dante may be considered as the bridge

thrown over the stream of time, which unites the modern 225
and ancient world. The distorted notions of invisible
things which Dante and his rival Milton have idealised,
are merely the mask and the mantle in which these great
poets walk through eternity enveloped and disguised. It
is a difficult question to determine how far they were 230
conscious of the distinction which must have subsisted in
their minds between their own creeds and that of the
people. Dante at least appears to wish to mark the full
extent of it by placing Riphæus, whom Virgil calls
justissimus unus, in Paradise, and observing a most heretical 235
caprice in his distribution of rewards and punishments.
And Milton's poem contains within itself a philosophical
refutation of that system of which, by a strange and
natural antithesis, it has been a chief popular support.
Nothing can exceed the energy and magnificence of the 240
character of Satan as expressed in *Paradise Lost*. It is a
mistake to suppose that he could ever have been intended
for the popular personification of evil. Implacable hate,
patient cunning, and a sleepless refinement of device to
inflict the extremest anguish on an enemy, these things 245
are evil; and, although venial in a slave, are not to be
forgiven in a tyrant; although redeemed by much that
ennobles his defeat in one subdued, are marked by all
that dishonours his conquest in the victor. Milton's Devil
as a moral being is as far superior to his God, as one who 250
perseveres in some purpose which he has conceived to be
excellent in spite of adversity and torture, is to one who
in the cold security of undoubted triumph inflicts the
most horrible revenge upon his enemy, not from any
mistaken notion of inducing him to repent of a persever- 255
ance in enmity, but with the alleged design of exasperating
him to deserve new torments. Milton has so far violated

the popular creed (if this shall be judged to be a violation)
as to have alleged no superiority of moral virtue to his
god over his devil. And this bold neglect of a direct moral 260
purpose is the most decisive proof of the supremacy of
Milton's genius. He mingled as it were the elements of
human nature as colours upon a single pallet, and arranged
them in the composition of his great picture according to
the laws of epic truth, that is, according to the laws of that 265
principle by which a series of actions of the external
universe and of intelligent and ethical beings is calculated
to excite the sympathy of succeeding generations of
mankind. . . . All high poetry is infinite; it is as the first 270
acorn, which contained all oaks potentially. Veil after veil
may be undrawn, and the inmost naked beauty of the
meaning never exposed. A great poem is a fountain for
ever overflowing with the waters of wisdom and delight;
and after one person and one age has exhausted all its 275
divine effluence which their peculiar relations enable them
to share, another and yet another succeeds, and new relations are ever developed, the source of an unforeseen and
an unconceived delight. . . .

But poets have been challenged to resign the civic crown 280
to reasoners and mechanists, on another plea. It is admitted
that the exercise of the imagination is most delightful,
but it is alleged that that of reason is more useful. Let us
examine, as the grounds of this distinction, what is here
meant by utility. Pleasure or good, in a general sense, is 285
that which the consciousness of a sensitive and intelligent
being seeks, and in which, when found, it acquiesces.
There are two kinds of pleasure, one durable, universal
and permanent; the other transitory and particular.
Utility may either express the means of producing the 290
former or the latter. In the former sense, whatever

strengthens and purifies the affections, enlarges the imagination, and adds spirit to sense, is useful. But a narrower meaning may be assigned to the word utility, confining it to express that which banishes the importunity 295 of the wants of our animal nature, the surrounding men with security of life, the dispersing the grosser delusions of superstition, and the conciliating such a degree of mutual forbearance among men as may consist with the motives of personal advantage.   300

Undoubtedly the promoters of utility, in this limited sense, have their appointed office in society. They follow the footsteps of poets, and copy the sketches of their creations into the book of common life. They make space, and give time. Their exertions are of the highest value, 305 so long as they confine their administration of the concerns of the inferior powers of our nature within the limits due to the superior ones. But while the sceptic destroys gross superstitions, let him spare to deface, as some of the French writers have defaced, the eternal truths charactered 310 upon the imaginations of men. Whilst the mechanist abridges, and the political economist combines, labour, let them beware that their speculations, for want of correspondence with those first principles which belong to the imagination, do not tend, as they have in modern England, 315 to exasperate at once the extremes of luxury and want. They have exemplified the saying, 'To him that hath, more shall be given; and from him that hath not, the little that he hath shall be taken away.' The rich have become richer, and the poor have become poorer; and the vessel of 320 the state is driven between the Scylla and Charybdis of anarchy and despotism. Such are the effects which must ever flow from an unmitigated exercise of the calculating faculty.

It is difficult to define pleasure in its highest sense; 325
the definition involving a number of apparent paradoxes.
For, from an inexplicable defect of harmony in the constitution of human nature, the pain of the inferior is
frequently connected with the pleasures of the superior
portions of our being. Sorrow, terror, anguish, despair 330
itself, are often the chosen expressions of an approximation
to the highest good. Our sympathy in tragic fiction depends on this principle; tragedy delights by affording a
shadow of that pleasure which exists in pain. This is the
source also of the melancholy which is inseparable from 335
the sweetest melody. The pleasure that is in sorrow is
sweeter than the pleasure of pleasure itself. And hence
the saying, 'It is better to go to the house of mourning
than to the house of mirth.' Not that this highest species
of pleasure is necessarily linked with pain. The delight 340
of love and friendship, the ecstacy of the admiration of
nature, the joy of the perception and still more of the
creation of poetry, is often wholly unalloyed.

The production and assurance of pleasure in this highest
sense is true utility. Those who produce and preserve 345
this pleasure are poets or poetical philosophers. . . .

We have more moral, political, and historical wisdom,
than we know how to reduce into practice; we have more
scientific and economical knowledge than can be accom-
modated to the just distribution of the produce which it 350
multiples. The poetry, in these systems of thought, is concealed by the accumulation of facts and calculating processes. There is no want of knowledge respecting what is
wisest and best in morals, government, and political
economy, or at least what is wiser and better than what 355
men now practise and endure. But we let '*I dare not* wait
upon *I would*, like the poor cat in the adage.' We want the

creative faculty to imagine that which we know; we want
the generous impulse to act that which we imagine; we
want the poetry of life: our calculations have outrun con- 360
ception; we have eaten more than we can digest. The
cultivation of those sciences which have enlarged the limits
of the empire of man over the external world, has, for
want of the poetical faculty, proportionally circumscribed
those of the internal world; and man, having enslaved the 365
elements, remains himself a slave. To what but a cultivation of the mechanical arts in a degree disproportioned to
the presence of the creative faculty, which is the basis of
all knowledge, is to be attributed the abuse of all invention
for abridging and combining labour, to the exasperation 370
of the inequality of mankind? From what other cause
has it arisen that the discoveries which should have
lightened, have added a weight to the curse imposed on
Adam? Poetry, and the principle of Self, of which money
is the visible incarnation, are the God and Mammon of the 375
world. . . .

Poetry is indeed something divine. It is at once the
centre and circumference of knowledge; it is that which
comprehends all science, and that to which all science must
be referred. It is at the same time the root and blossom 380
of all other systems of thought; it is that from which all
spring, and that which adorns all; and that which, if
blighted, denies the fruit and the seed, and withholds
from the barren world the nourishment and the succession
of the scions of the tree of life. It is the perfect and con- 385
summate surface and bloom of all things; it is as the odour
and the colour of the rose to the texture of the elements
which compose it, as the form and splendour of unfaded
beauty to the secrets of anatomy and corruption. What
were virtue, love, patriotism, friendship,—what were the 390

scenery of this beautiful universe which we inhabit; what
were our consolations on this side of the grave—and what
were our aspirations beyond it, if poetry did not ascend to
bring light and fire from those eternal regions where the
owl-winged faculty of calculation dare not ever soar? 395
Poetry is not like reasoning, a power to be exerted according to the determination of the will. A man cannot say,
'I will compose poetry.' The greatest poet even cannot
say it; for the mind in creation is as a fading coal, which
some invisible influence, like an inconstant wind, awakens 400
to transitory brightness; this power arises from within,
like the colour of a flower which fades and changes as it is
developed, and the conscious portions of our nature are
unprophetic either of its approach or its departure. Could
this influence be durable in its original purity and force, 405
it is impossible to predict the greatness of the results;
but when composition begins, inspiration is already on the
decline, and the most glorious poetry that has ever been
communicated to the world is probably a feeble shadow of
the original conceptions of the poet. I appeal to the 410
greatest poets of the present day, whether it is not an error
to assert that the finest passages of poetry are produced by
labour and study. The toil and the delay recommended by
critics, can be justly interpreted to mean no more than a
careful observation of the inspired moments, and an 415
artificial connection of the spaces between their sugges-
tions, by the intertexture of conventional expressions; a
necessity only imposed by the limitedness of the poetical
faculty itself: for Milton conceived the Paradise Lost as a
whole before he executed it in portions. We have his own 420
authority also for the muse having 'dictated' to him the
'unpremeditated song.' And let this be an answer to
those who would allege the fifty-six various readings of the

first line of the Orlando Furioso. Compositions so produced are to poetry what mosaic is to painting. The 425
instinct and intuition of the poetical faculty is still more
observable in the plastic and pictorial arts: a great statue
or picture grows under the power of the artist as a child in
the mother's womb; and the very mind which directs the
hands in formation, is incapable of accounting to itself 430
for the origin, the gradations, or the media of the process.

Poetry is the record of the best and happiest moments
of the happiest and best minds. We are aware of evanescent visitations of thought and feeling, sometimes associated with place or person, sometimes regarding our own 435
mind alone, and always arising unforeseen and depart-
ing unbidden, but elevating and delightful beyond
all expression: so that even in the desire and the regret
they leave, there cannot but be pleasure, participating as
it does in the nature of its object. It is as it were the inter- 440
penetration of a diviner nature through our own; but its
footsteps are like those of a wind over the sea, which the
coming calm erases, and whose traces remain only, as on
the wrinkled sand which paves it. These and corresponding conditions of being are experienced principally by 445
those of the most delicate sensibility and the most enlarged
imagination; and the state of mind produced by them is
at war with every base desire. The enthusiasm of virtue,
love, patriotism, and friendship, is essentially linked with
such emotions; and whilst they last, self appears as what it 450
is, an atom to a universe. Poets are not only subject to
these experiences as spirits of the most refined organization, but they can colour all that they combine with the
evanescent hues of this ethereal world; a word, a trait in
the representation of a scene or a passion, will touch the 455
enchanted chord, and reanimate, in those who have ever

experienced those emotions, the sleeping, the cold, the buried image of the past. Poetry thus makes immortal all that is best and most beautiful in the world; it arrests the vanishing apparitions which haunt the interlunations of 460 life, and veiling them, or in language or in form, sends them forth among mankind, bearing sweet news of kindred joy to those with whom their sisters abide—abide, because there is no portal of expression from the caverns of the spirit which they inhabit into the universe of things. Poetry 465 redeems from decay the visitations of the divinity in man.

Poetry turns all things to loveliness; it exalts the beauty of that which is most beautiful, and it adds beauty to that which is most deformed; it marries exultation and horror, grief and pleasure, eternity and change; it subdues 470 to union, under its light yoke, all irreconcilable things. It transmutes all that it touches, and every form moving within the radiance of its presence is changed by wondrous sympathy to an incarnation of the spirit which it breathes: its secret alchemy turns to potable gold the 475 poisonous waters which flow from death through life; it strips the veil of familiarity from the world, and lays bare the naked and sleeping beauty, which is the spirit of its forms.

All things exist as they are perceived; at least in relation to the percipient. 'The mind is its own place, and of itself 480 can make a heaven of hell, a hell of heaven.' But poetry defeats the curse which binds us to be subjected to the accident of surrounding impressions. And whether it spreads its own figured curtain, or withdraws life's dark veil from before the scene of things, it equally creates for 485 us a being within our being. It makes us the inhabitant of a world to which the familiar world is a chaos. It reproduces the common universe of which we are portions and percipients, and it purges from our inward sight the

film of familiarity which obscures from us the wonder of 490
our being. It compels us to feel that which we perceive,
and to imagine that which we know. It creates anew the
universe, after it has been annihilated in our minds by the
recurrence of impressions blunted by reiteration. It
justifies the bold and true word of Tasso: *Non merita nome* 495
di creatore, se non Iddio ed il Poeta.

A poet, as he is the author to others of the highest
wisdom, pleasure, virtue and glory, so he ought personally
to be the happiest, the best, the wisest, and the most
illustrious of men. As to his glory, let time be challenged 500
to declare whether the fame of any other institutor of
human life be comparable to that of a poet. That he is
the wisest, the happiest, and the best, inasmuch as he is a
poet, is equally incontrovertible: the greatest poets have
been men of the most spotless virtue, of the most con- 505
summate prudence, and, if we would look into the interior
of their lives, the most fortunate of men: and the exceptions, as they regard those who possessed the poetic faculty
in a high yet inferior degree, will be found on considera-
tion to confine rather than destroy the rule. Let us for a 510
moment stoop to the arbitration of popular breath, and
usurping and uniting in our own persons the incompatible
characters of accuser, witness, judge and executioner, let
us decide without trial, testimony, or form, that certain
motives of those who are 'there sitting where we dare not 515
soar,' are reprehensible. Let as assume that Homer was
a drunkard, that Virgil was a flatterer, that Horace was a
coward, that Tasso was a madman, that Lord Bacon was
a peculator, that Raphael was a libertine, that Spenser was
a poet laureate. It is inconsistent with this division of our 520
subject to cite living poets, but posterity has done ample
justice to the great names now referred to. Their errors

have been weighed and found to have been dust in the
balance; if their sins 'were as scarlet, they are now white
as snow': they have been washed in the blood of the 525
mediator and redeemer, time. Observe in what a ludicrous
chaos the imputations of real or fictitious crime have been
confused in the contemporary calumnies against poetry
and poets; consider how little is, as it appears—or appears,
as it is; look to your own motives, and judge not, lest ye 530
be judged.

Poetry, as has been said, differs in this respect from
logic, that it is not subject to the control of the active
powers of the mind, and that its birth and recurrence have
no necessary connection with the consciousness or will. 535
It is presumptuous to determine that these are the necessary
conditions of all mental causation, when mental effects are
experienced insusceptible of being referred to them. The
frequent recurrence of the poetical power, it is obvious to
suppose, may produce in the mind a habit of order and 540
harmony correlative with its own nature and with its
effects upon other minds. But in the intervals of inspiration, and they may be frequent without being durable, a
poet becomes a man, and is abandoned to the sudden reflux
of the influences under which others habitually live. But 545
as he is more delicately organized than other men, and
sensible to pain and pleasure, both his own and that of
others, in a degree unknown to them, he will avoid the
one and pursue the other with an ardour proportioned to
this difference. And he renders himself obnoxious to 550
calumny, when he neglects to observe the circumstances
under which these objects of universal pursuit and flight
have disguised themselves in one another's garments.

But there is nothing necessarily evil in this error, and
thus cruelty, envy, revenge, avarice, and the passions 555

purely evil, have never formed any portion of the popular imputations on the lives of poets. . . .

In spite of the low-thoughted envy which would undervalue contemporary merit, our own will be a memorable age in intellectual achievements, and we live among such philosophers and poets as surpass beyond comparison any who have appeared since the last national struggle for civil and religious liberty. The most unfailing herald, companion, and follower of the awakening of a great people to work a beneficial change in opinion or institution, is poetry. At such periods there is an accumulation of the power of communicating and receiving intense and impassioned conceptions respecting man and nature. The persons in whom this power resides, may often, as far as regards many portions of their nature, have little apparent correspondence with that spirit of good of which they are the ministers. But even whilst they deny and abjure, they are yet compelled to serve, the power which is seated on the throne of their own soul. It is impossible to read the compositions of the most celebrated writers of the present day without being startled with the electric life which burns within their words. They measure the circumference and sound the depths of human nature with a comprehensive and all-penetrating spirit, and they are themselves perhaps the most sincerely astonished at its manifestations; for it is less their spirit than the spirit of the age. Poets are the hierophants of an unapprehended inspiration; the mirrors of the gigantic shadows which futurity casts upon the present; the words which express what they understand not; the trumpets which sing to battle and feel not what they inspire; the influence which is moved not, but moves. Poets are the unacknowledged legislators of the world.

APPENDIX A

(1) SOME gentlemen have affected to call the principles upon which this work and the former part of *Rights of Man* are founded, 'a new fangled doctrine.' The question is not whether those principles are new or old, but whether they are right or wrong. Suppose the former, I will shew their effect by a figure easily understood.

It is now towards the middle of February. Were I to take a turn into the country, the trees would present a leafless winterly appearance. As people are apt to pluck twigs as they walk along, I perhaps might do the same, and by chance might observe, that a *single bud* on that twig had begun to swell. I should reason very unnaturally, or rather not reason at all, to suppose *this* was the *only* bud in England which had this appearance. Instead of deciding thus, I should instantly conclude, that the same appearance was beginning, or about to begin, every where; and though the vegetable sleep will continue longer on some trees and plants than on others, and though some of them may not *blossom* for two or three years, all will be in leaf in the summer, except those which are *rotten*. What pace the political summer may keep with the natural, no human foresight can determine. It is, however, not difficult to perceive that the spring is begun.

(Thomas Paine, *Rights of Man. Part the Second*, 1792)

(2) Many well-meaning persons may think that the attainment of the good which I propose as the ultimatum of philanthropic exertion is visionary and inconsistent with human nature; they would tell me not to make people happy for fear of overstocking the world. . . . But when the philosopher

and philanthropist contemplates the universe, when he per-
ceives existing evils that admit of amendment, and hears tell
of other evils, which, in the course of sixty centuries, may
again derange the system of happiness which the amendment
is calculated to produce, does he submit to prolong a positive
evil, because if that were eradicated . . . another evil would
take [its] place [?]

To how contemptible a degradation of grossest credulity
will not prejudice lower the human mind! We see in winter
that the foliage of the trees is gone, that they present to the
view nothing but leafless branches—we see that the loveliness
of the flower decays, though the root continues in the earth.
What opinion should we form of that man who, when he
walked in the freshness of spring, beheld the fields enamelled
with flowers, and the foliage bursting from the buds, should
find fault with all this beautiful order, and murmur his dis-
contents because winter must come, and the landscape be
robbed of its beauty for a while again? Yet this man is Mr.
Malthus. Do we not see that the laws of nature perpetually
act by disorganization and reproduction, each alternately
becoming cause and effect [?] The analogies that we can draw
from physical to moral topics are of all others the most
striking.

(Shelley, *Proposals for an Association,* &c., 1812)

APPENDIX B

For the authors of those great poems which we admire do not attain to excellence through the rules of any art but they utter their beautiful melodies of verse in a state of inspiration and, as it were, *possessed* by a spirit not their own. Thus the composers of lyrical poetry create those admired songs of theirs in a state of divine insanity, like the Corybantes,[1] who lose all control over their reason in the enthusiasm of the sacred dance; and, during this supernatural possession, are excited to the rhythm and harmony which they communicate to men; like the Bacchantes who, when possessed by the God, draw honey and milk from the rivers in which, when they come to their senses, they find nothing but simple water. For the souls of the poets, as poets tell us, have this peculiar ministration in the world. They tell us that these souls, flying like bees from flower to flower and wandering over the gardens and the meadows and the honey-flowing fountains of the Muses, return to us laden with the sweetness of melody; and arrayed as they are in the plumes of rapid imagination they speak truth. For a poet is indeed a thing ethereally light, winged, and sacred, nor can he compose anything worth calling poetry until he becomes inspired and as it were mad; or whilst any reason remains in him.

(From Plato's *Ion*, translated by Shelley)

[1] *Corybantes:* dancing followers of Cybele (goddess of Nature).

NOTES

PAGE 53. MUTABILITY.

5–8. The Aeolian or wind harp (Aeolus was god of the winds) made unearthly swelling and ebbing chords when wedged in a tree or window, suggesting the music of Nature herself, or divine inspiration (see *A Defence of Poetry*, p. 168).

5. *dissonant*: variously-sounding.

PAGE 54. Stanzas from LAON AND CYTHNA. *Laon and Cythna; or, The Revolution of the Golden City*, a narrative poem of twelve cantos in Spenserian stanzas, was the original version of *The Revolt of Islam*. The revisions, however, involved little more than changing the words 'God' and 'Christ', and suppressing the theme of incest.

Plan. An introduction (Canto I) shows Good (a snake) and Evil (an eagle) in symbolic conflict. Laon and Cythna are childhood lovers in Greece (II). Abducted for the Turkish monarch's seraglio (III), Cythna leads a successful popular revolt in Constantinople (IV–V); but the new régime is bloodily suppressed by foreign troops, and Cythna rescues Laon from the massacre. During a brief idyll together (VI), she recounts her adventures (VII–VIII), and encourages his hopes for the future (IX). [This extract is from Canto IX, stanzas 21–25.] Meanwhile plague and famine, following the tyrant's reprisals, make the priests seek a human sacrifice to propitiate their God (X). Laon gives himself up to buy Cythna's safe-conduct to America (XI), but she comes to share his fiery death; and they are united in a 'Temple of the Spirit', from which the struggle for human liberty is perpetually renewed (XII).

Despite the Turkish setting, the parallel with foreign intervention against revolutionary France is intended to be close. Cythna, who speaks the lines chosen to Laon, is an idealization of Shelley's wife Mary, to whom the poem was dedicated. For the symbolism of the seasons, see Appendix A(1).

32–34. *The moon . . . pray*: neglected science is waning like a moon, and superstition flourishes instead.

35. *blast*: pestilential air.

39. *frore*: frozen.

40–43. *Spring . . . sunrise*: the antecedent of *shade* is *promise*; *future* is the subject of *flings*. 'Freedom will come, though we must die who made its coming possible—its coming which is like a shadow thrown by the light of the future (or like our own deaths that are really an assurance of future triumph).'

PAGE 55. OZYMANDIAS. Probably written in friendly rivalry with Horace Smith, whose sonnet 'On a Stupendous Leg of Granite' appeared in Hunt's *Examiner* three weeks after Shelley's. The 'traveller' was most likely a book, Pococke's illustrated *A Description of the East* (1743), which supplied features from several ruined statues near Thebes (Luxor) in Egypt, especially those of Memnon and Rameses II ('Osymandias', in Greek). The latter once bore the inscription: 'I am the king of kings, Osymandias—if any one would know how great I am, and where I lie, let him exceed the works that I have done.'

6–8. *those passions . . . fed*: carved on the dead stone, his passions have outlasted the sculptor's hand that copied (and derided) them, and his own heart that nourished them.

PAGE 56. PROMETHEUS UNBOUND. Interpretation of Shelley's greatest completed work has been confused by the idea that it is all 'a drama in the mind'—an idea deriving from Mary Shelley's mistaken but influential note: 'Shelley believed that mankind had only to will that there should be no evil, and there would be none.' What he did say was that if, for example, the revolutionary doctrines of Jesus were acted upon, all political and religious institutions would be overthrown, and 'man exempt from the external evils of his own choice would be left free to struggle with the physical evils which exist in spite of him'. This is an exact synopsis of *Prometheus Unbound*. The fact that 'external evils' are set up or tolerated by man's own will does not make the evils themselves mental, nor does it make them simply disappear when men renounce them.

Plan. Act I. Prometheus, undergoing physical torture, but attended by two Ocean nymphs, sisters of Asia, withdraws his Curse on Jupiter, who, exasperated, tortures him mentally by reminding him of how individual and social attempts to better the lot of mankind have alike failed. Earth comforts her son with counter-thoughts of good.

Act II. Prometheus's exiled wife Asia is drawn by the obscure sympathetic forces of destiny to the cave of Demogorgon, so releasing the Hour of Jupiter's overthrow.

Act III. Jupiter was expecting his own child (perhaps symbolizing the Malthusian doctrine that over-population would always prevent human betterment: see Appendix A(2)) to make his dominion over man permanent; but it is Demogorgon who arrives with the appointed Hour and overthrows him. The world is liberated; Prometheus and Asia, reunited, will devote themselves henceforth to art and science.

Act IV, an appendix of universal rejoicing, added later, is interesting in its scientific symbolism, but except for one or two lyrics is decidedly the weakest section poetically.

These events take place concurrently on three symbolic levels:

(1) *Natural.* A quiescent volcano (Demogorgon's cave) is invaded by the sea (the Ocean nymphs) and erupts, causing both destruction and regeneration.

(2) *Political.* The people (Demogorgon as agent of Destiny), when equipped with a humane ideology (Asia), enter into their historical role (Demogorgon as Destiny itself) by overthrowing their oppressors (Jupiter) and freeing humanity (Prometheus) through social revolution.

(3) *Moral.* Man (Prometheus) renounces vengeance (the Curse, standing for all wrong moral attitudes), and so by means of Love (Asia) eliminates those evils from the world that result from Man's misguided will and are therefore in his power to eliminate (Jupiter).

Characters. The main characters (except Demogorgon) and the myth are borrowed from Aeschylus's *Prometheus Bound*, the surviving play of a trilogy in which the Titan, Prometheus, having helped Zeus to achieve power, is riveted to a rock with an eagle eating his liver for having also championed the human race against Zeus. Later he was to have bought his release by yielding up the secret that a child born of Jupiter's union with Thetis would supplant him. But Shelley 'was averse from a catastrophe [= conclusion] so feeble as that of reconciling the Champion with the Oppressor of mankind'. The characters are not simple allegories and must not be 'translated' too narrowly. *Jupiter* is the collective 'external evil' that men have imposed on themselves, including monarchy, capitalism, and religion. *Prometheus* represents man at his highest point of development, intellectual, moral, and political. *Asia*, his wife, is the vital essence of Nature, as well as the Ideal that seeks to express itself through Nature. *Panthea* and *Ione* are lesser aspects of their 'great sister' (they have been identified as Hope and Memory, but exact labels are unconvincing). *Demogorgon* (the new element in the myth) is both the principle of historical change (Necessity), and the means through which it acts (the people). He lives in a volcano, and erupts when the Sea Sisters reach his domain. Volcanoes erupt when penetrated by the sea: a scientific metaphor for saying that the popular power becomes irresistible when Love co-operates with Historical Necessity.

The drama was not for the stage; and it is 'undramatic' in its avoidance of causality. Shelley does not want to say that renouncing vengeance, &c., will automatically *cause* Jupiter's permanent removal, only that this is an essential condition of it. Nor does the poem suggest a programme of action (this is outlined elsewhere, in prose), but tries to prepare men's imaginations by showing them 'what ought to be, or may be'.

The Curse uttered on Jupiter was valuable ('a treasured spell') as long as there was nothing else Prometheus could do but express defiance (corresponding to the immaturity of the Reform movement in Shelley's day). Its withdrawal now that experience has matured him is a renunciation not of force (Jupiter is still overthrown forcibly), but of *revenge*, which always opens the way to the return of tyranny (see note to ll. 292-3).

The commonest criticisms, that Jupiter falls too easily, and that perfection follows too fast, are baseless. Jupiter's doom is inevitable, but he goes down fighting, in a contest which shakes the planets (this understandably happens offstage, as in Greek drama). And the prolonged period during which 'veil by veil, evil and error fall' is foreshortened for dramatic reasons, just as are Prometheus's countless years of torment in Act I.

2. *One*: Prometheus himself. The *Monarch* addressed is Jupiter.

9. *eyeless in hate*: blind with hatred (goes with *thou*, l. 10).

15. Stressed: *Scórn and despáir,—thése are míne émpire.*

28. *Shadow*: image, copy.

34. *wingèd hound*: the eagle, more venomous by contact with Jupiter than by its own nature.

59. *recall*: remember.

65. *without beams*: without the 'rays' caused by atmospheric moisture.

82–83. *I had . . . own*: all colours derive from the sun. The Voices are of the four elements: earth, water, upper (fiery) atmosphere, air.

121. *frore*: frozen.

124. *informs*: fills.

137. *And love*: 'And that thou lovest me'.

192. *Zoroaster*: chief of the wise men (Magi) of ancient Persia. This story about him is unexplained.

195. *of life and death*: i.e. of life, and of death. This underworld of duplicates (*shadows*) is perhaps that of intellectual abstraction, containing mental copies—thoughts—of all that exists or could exist. Prometheus *imagines* Jupiter repeating 'that which may be evil' (the moral equivalent of playing back a recording of it).

208. Heavily stressed: *Ańd hé, the Supréme Týrant, thróned.*

212. *Hades*: Greek name for Pluto, god of the underworld. *Typhon*: a monster suppressed by Jupiter.

224–6. *Yet . . . sounds*: i.e. 'A Shape . . . appears, a throng of sounds . . . arise[s]' (attracted into the plural by *sounds*).

229. *our sweet sister*: Asia.

236. *stay*: support.

292–3. *Heap . . . good*: Milton's God had allowed Satan to rise from the lake of Hell, deliberately intending

> That with reiterated crimes he might
> Heap on himself damnation.
> (*Paradise Lost*, I. 210–15)

Prometheus is renouncing such cruelty, which Shelley thought unforgivable. (Note how, in ll. 302–11, the Curse is repudiated in its own stanza-form.)

294–5. *Both . . . solitude*: 'May both be infinite—yourself (doing evil), and your agonizing isolation (seeing good in others). (Latin: 'Et . . . et'.)

324. *serpent-cinctured wand*: staff twined with snakes, emblem of Mercury, messenger of the gods.

326. *hydra tresses*: 'hair' consisting of heads. The Hydra was a many-headed water-snake killed by Hercules.

330. *clanging*: screaming harshly.

342. *Son of Maia*: Mercury himself, son of Maia and Jupiter.

345. *streams of fire and wail*: Phlegethon and Cocytus, two rivers of Hades.

346–7. *Geryon . . . Gorgon . . . Chimaera . . . Sphinx*: monsters of Greek mythology. Oedipus's liberation of Thebes from the Sphinx led him into unwitting marriage with his own mother (*unnatural love*), and into cursing his two sons to make them kill one another (*more unnatural hate*).

351. *We die with our desire*: 'we are nothing but embodied lust for cruelty, and die if it is thwarted'.

359. *So*: to such a degree.

371. *a secret*: that Jupiter's son by Thetis would overthrow him.

386. *my belovèd race*: mankind.

387. *thought-executing*: (*a*) carrying out orders as fast as thought; (*b*) 'beheading thought', i.e. penalizing opinion.

396. *that fatal word*: the secret of l. 371.

398. *the Sicilian*: Damocles, forced to dine under a sword hanging by a hair, illustrating how kings live in fear.

405. *Too much . . . err*: the wretchedness of being an evil-doer is itself punishment enough.

408. *fear delay*: irony: Prometheus does not fear the indefinite 'delay' of his own release from torture.

429. *Pity . . . Heaven*: more irony: 'Save your pity for yourself!'

461–2. *But why . . . deep?* A legion of Furies is more hideous than the sum of its parts.

466. *so are we*: i.e. glad.

479. *lidless*: unclosed.

484. *animal life*: living nerves (Lat. *animalis*, of the nerves).

527. *rapt us*: carried us away.

546. *One*: Jesus, whose 'words' only were taken up by the Church. The cities vomiting smoke are burning in religious wars (*kindled* is an ironic pun).

565. *his*: Prometheus's (the *thee* of ll. 561–3).

566. *a little respite*: ironical: the coming vision of social disaster is no less agonizing than that of Christ on the cross.

567. *a disenchanted Nation*: France (Coleridge's phrase in *France: An Ode*). *disenchanted*: released from an evil spell.

572. *another's*: i.e. hatred's—the ideals of the Revolution are lost in the bloodshed of internal struggles.

594. *an emblem*: Jesus on the cross.

609. *ounces*: hunting-leopards (*hooded* until released at their prey).

618–19. *terror . . . gorged*: superstitious fear lingers in every man's mind after he has stopped believing in the causes of it. *ravin*: prey, spoil.

622. *fanes*: temples.

631. *they . . . do*: a cruelly ironical echo of Jesus's words on the cross (Luke xxiii. 34).

646–7. *There are . . . one*: 'Don't make me suffer the same pain twice by describing what I saw.'

658–61. *those subtle . . . ether*: these 'counter-Furies' represent (roughly): (1) Liberty (2) Self-sacrifice (3) Political philosophy (4) Poetry (5) and (6) Hope and Despair.

682. *liquid*: clear.

752. *two shapes*: Hope and Despair, twin opposites. Hope recognizes Love, with Venus on his helmet; Despair adds that Love and Pain are inseparable, and easily confused.

772. *Desolation*:

'Homer says, that the Goddess Calamity is delicate . . . "Her feet are soft", he says, "for she treads not upon the ground, but makes her path upon the heads of men" . . . The same evidence is sufficient to make manifest the tenderness of Love. For Love walks not upon the earth, nor over the heads of men, which are not indeed very soft; but he dwells within, and treads on the softest of existing things. . . .'
                    (Shelley's translation of Plato's *Symposium*)

804. *responses*: echoes in the mind (stressed: *résponses*).

807. *air-born*: born of air, i.e. created by the mind.

814. *Though I should dream*: 'Even at the cost of dreaming'.

FROM ACT II, SCENE I. Asia and Panthea are nearing the realm of Demogorgon. He is creative as well as destructive, and his neighbourhood is exuberantly fertile, like the region of volcanic fall-out round Naples on which the scenery is based, the traditional locality of the war between Jupiter and the Titans.

8. *drifted*: a participle: 'wafted', 'made to drift'.

10. *hangs . . . flowers*: i.e. hangs a pearl in each flower.

12–13. *And bends . . . anemone*: an inversion: 'save where one anemone bends and fades . . .'.

14–15. The plural verbs after *many a one* were deliberate.

18. *it*: the star.

38. *lake-surrounded flute*: flute-music heard over encircling water.

41–63. This extended image expresses the way in which historical change and its human agents (reformers, poets) interact. These agents (*the destined*) are roused from their empty chatter or apathy (*talk or slumber*) by delightful intimations (*echoes music-tongued*) of the task they must accomplish. Destiny inspires them and lures them on, as mountains attract clouds. But they are driven as well as attracted; in following their own wishes they are obeying the dictate of historical necessity (see Introduction, p. 37).

53. *plume-uplifting wind*: volcanic vapour raising a plume of steam as it is emitted from Demogorgon's cave. (See p. 37.)

62. *fatal mountain*: mountain of destiny.

FROM ACT II, SCENE V. *Voice in the Air, Singing*: the 'voice' is Panthea's, but Prometheus is really addressing Asia through her lips.

4. *them*: themselves.

8. *vest*: vesture, robe.

16. *that liquid splendour*: the 'atmosphere divinest' surrounding her.

21. *of whom*: of those whom.

PAGE 92. THE MASK OF ANARCHY. On 16 August 1819, some 60,000 working men, women, and children assembled on vacant land adjoining St. Peter's Church, Manchester, to demonstrate for Parliamentary Reform. When 'Orator' Hunt began speaking, the Yeomanry (mounted militia representing the local employers) went in with drawn sabres to arrest him. They were not all sober (ll. 48–49), and when they got into difficulties, a detachment of regular cavalry was ordered to charge the unarmed crowd. Then, a witness said, 'swords were up and swords were down': eleven people were killed and about 500 injured (100 were women), and with savage derision the massacre was dubbed 'Peterloo', after the recent Battle of Waterloo.

A fortnight after 'a voice from over the sea' had reached Shelley at Leghorn he told his publisher: 'the torrent of my indignation has not yet done boiling in my veins'. He sent the poem to Leigh Hunt on 23 September for *The Examiner*; but Hunt dared not print it until 1832—after the Reform Bill had been passed. 'The poem was written for the people', as Mary Shelley said; and it draws its hard-hitting eloquence from the contemporary street ballad as well as from the popular tradition of Biblical radicalism handed down from Commonwealth days. *Mask*, in the title, means 'masque', pageant, but here contains a bitter pun.

Plan. As Anarchy, unleashed by the governing classes, overruns England (ll. 1–85), Hope throws herself in its path (ll. 86–101), allowing the spirit of human freedom and solidarity (ll. 102–21) to reaffirm itself (ll. 122–38), as if the very soil were appealing to men (ll. 139–end).

6. *Castlereagh*: Foreign Secretary and Leader of the Commons, bitterly hated by the common people in his own day.

8. *Seven bloodhounds*: the seven states (Austria, Bourbon France, Portugal, Prussia, Russia, Spain, Sweden) which, with England, agreed in 1815 to postpone indefinitely the abolition of the slave trade.

15. *Eldon*: Lord Eldon, rich and reactionary Lord Chancellor, notorious for weeping in public. The *ermined gown* is his judge's robe.

18–21. i.e. affecting a concern for children (e.g. by taking Shelley's away from him), he really destroyed their understanding.

22–23. *Clothed . . . night*: 'Clothed with the Bible and with darkness, as if with light,' i.e. enveloped in moral darkness masquerading as piety. Viscount Sidmouth, Home Secretary, had in 1818 secured a Commons vote of a million pounds to build more churches for the new industrial population.

30–33. 'And I looked, and behold a pale horse: and his name that sat on him was Death, and Hell followed with him. And power was given unto them over the fourth part of the earth, to kill with sword, and with hunger, and with the beasts of the earth' (Revelation vi. 8).

82–83. *So . . . Tower*: Habeas Corpus had been suspended in 1817 on the pretext of a plot to seize the Bank of England and the Tower of London. A put-up job, Shelley suggests.

110. *a Shape*: the Shape is partly snake, symbolizing resistance to oppression, and partly Venus, affirming the bond of blood between men (*crimson dew*).

176. *the Ghost of Gold*: paper money: a swindle, Shelley thought, for increasing the exploitation of labour.

197–208. *Birds . . . none*: 'The foxes have holes, and the birds of the air have nests; but the Son of man hath not where to lay his head' (Matthew viii. 20).

220. *Fame*: rumour.

221–4. *For . . . home*: the clauses dovetail: 'For the labourer returned from his work, freedom means bread and a table spread in a happy home.'

244–5. *when all . . . Gaul*: the alliance of 1793 against revolutionary France.

251. *him following Christ*: Zacchaeus (Luke xix. 1–10).

256–7. *whence they . . . prey*: 'from which they had derived the class-privileges they now sought to abolish'.

309. *loosening*: letting-loose, onrush.

320. *sphereless stars*: stars shooting from their spheres, i.e. meteors.

344–63. *And if then . . . company*: passive resistance is recommended at any future Peterloo,

. . . not because active resistance is not justifiable when all other means shall have failed, but because in this instance temperance and courage would produce greater advantages than the most decisive victory. . . . The soldier is a man and an Englishman. This unexpected reception would probably throw him back upon a recollection of the true nature of the measures of which he was made the instrument, and the enemy might be converted into the ally.

(*A Philosophical View of Reform*, 1819)

360. *bold, true warriors*: regular soldiers, as distinct from local militia whose interests necessarily clashed with those of the labouring classes.

365–6. *Shall steam . . . oracular*: ancient oracles were 'inspired' to eloquence by inhaling vapours from their volcanic caves.

PAGE 105. ODE TO THE WEST WIND. The pace and energy of this great 'fighting prayer' (ll. 51–52) are matched by its intellectual control. Three worlds combine in it: the *natural* (seasonal change); the *social* (revolution); and the *personal* (the poet's task). Stanzas 1–3 were written on 25 October 1819,

'in a wood that skirts the Arno, near Florence, and on a day when that tempestuous wind, whose temperature is at once mild and animating, was collecting the vapours which pour down the autumnal rains. They began, as I foresaw, at sunset with a violent tempest of hail and rain, attended with that magnificent thunder and lightning peculiar to the Cisalpine regions.' (Shelley's note.)

The Wind is not wind only, but the 'breath of Autumn's being'— the essence of seasonal change, symbolizing Change itself, including social change. But the Wind, in destroying the outworn, provides for the birth of the new. Stanzas 1–3 show this activity 'moving everywhere',

(1) on the earth: expelling the dead leaves and scattering the seeds of new life.

(2) in the air: assembling the cloud-cover, the 'dome' both of a sepulchre and of an energizing volcano-like storm.

(3) on and under the sea: rousing it from its over-idealized dreams of the past; subjecting underwater vegetation to the universal law.

The Wind of change acts both horizontally and vertically within each element: *stream/steep; flocks/feed in air; level/chasms*. In stanza 4, the poet longs for the simple passivity of leaf, cloud, and wave; or the irresponsibility of childhood. In stanza 5, he triumphantly accepts his adult humanity, demanding total possession by the Wind, to be made prophet of the very movement of change that must ultimately destroy his individual life (see Stanzas from *Laon and Cythna*, ll. 40–41, p. 55).

The *storm* (often in Shelley a crisis of renewal) links volcanic imagery of social revolution with Biblical imagery of resurrection. The seeds will rise from their graves when the spring wind blows its trumpet, just as, after 'black rain, and fire, and hail', mankind will be reborn at the trumpet-call of poetry.

4. *pale*: takes up the suggestion of *ghosts*; but the four colours glance at the four 'nations' of mankind: Far Eastern, African, European, American Indian.

9. *azure sister*: the Zephyrus (Favonius) of the poets, bringing blue skies. The autumnal west wind was Ausonius.

16–17. *Loose clouds . . . Ocean*: clouds form from the interaction (*tangled boughs*) of air and sea, which Shelley had seen literally 'tangled' in tree-shaped waterspouts on the Mediterranean. His syntax could also bear the meaning: 'Clouds are shed on the wind, as earthly leaves are shaken from the tangled boughs of the sky (treetops that "feed in air"), and of the sea (the "oozy woods" underwater).' (Cf. syntax of *The Mask of Anarchy*, ll. 221–4).

18. *Angels*: messengers, heralds (referring to *Loose clouds*).

19. *aery surge*: sea of air.

20. *bright hair uplifted*: the scene is in three dimensions, not two. Low, broken clouds are racing in the stream of the wind, while the whole upper sky slowly clouds over for the storm. The slow-moving *locks* of the storm (a precise image because 'cirrus' means 'lock of hair') are spread out on top of the turbulent lower air (on the wind's *blue surface*), and so are *uplifted* by it, like the hair of someone submerging in water, or of a wild dancer.

21. *Maenad*: female celebrant of Bacchus. Shelley had recently admired a Florentine relief showing 'four figures of Maenads under the inspiration of the God', whose divine intoxication seemed to have caught them

in its whirlwinds, and to bear them over the earth as the rapid volutions of a tempest bear the ever-changing trunk of a water-spout, as the torrent of a mountain river whirls the leaves in its full eddies. Their hair loose and floating seems caught in the tempest of their own tumultuous motion. . . . (See Introduction, p. 37, and Appendix B).

31. 'Made smooth by his own winding currents'.

32. *pumice*: porous volcanic lava. *Baiae's bay*: (pron. 'by-ee'), part of the Bay of Naples, a resort of the fashionable and the great under the Roman empire, but also a scene of luxury and cruelty. Hence the Wind must 'waken' the sea from its 'summer dreams' of Roman greatness.

33–36. And saw . . . them! The year before, Shelley had coasted along this bay over water

so translucent that you could see the hollow caverns clothed with the glaucous sea-moss, and the leaves and branches of those delicate weeds that pave the unequal bottom of the water. . . . After passing the Bay of Baiae, and observing the ruins of its antique grandeur standing like rocks in the transparent sea under our boat, we landed to visit lake Avernus. (Letter to Peacock, 22 December 1818.)

34. *intenser day*: clearer blue.

57. *Make me thy lyre*: See *A Defence of Poetry*, p. 168.

58. *What if . . . ?*: 'What does it matter if . . . ?'

63. *my dead thoughts*: especially *The Revolt of Islam*, which 'fell stillborn from the press' in 1818.

64. *a new birth*: the cycle of death and renewal had a personal urgency for Shelley, as his wife, childless since William's death, was now expecting another baby (b. 12 November).

70. *Winter . . . Spring*: See Appendix A(1).

PAGE 108. LOVE'S PHILOSOPHY. Shelley copied this playful lyric, an imitation of Anacreon, into the diary he gave Sophia Stacey, his uncle's ward, just after Christmas 1819. Written before he met Miss Stacey, the poem reflects a saying from Boccaccio, 'Lips don't lose their freshness by kissing, but are renewed like the moon,' which he felt 'might do some good to the common narrow-minded conceptions of love'. The title is probably Leigh Hunt's.

PAGE 109. ENGLAND IN 1819. Shelley sent this sonnet to Hunt on 23 December 1819, not expecting him to publish so bitter an attack on the prevailing social order. The title is Mary Shelley's.

1. George III was 81 and had been totally insane for nearly ten years.

7. refers to Peterloo, and carries a double indictment: those demonstrating in St. Peter's Fields were 'stabbed' on land which should have been cultivated to relieve their distress.

8–9. *An army . . . wield*: an army used for suppressing liberty and for private plunder might turn against its masters. It is made up of 'men and Englishmen', hence the personal pronoun *whom*. *Liberticide and prey* govern a singular verb.

10. *Golden and sanguine laws*: laws serving the interests of wealth and arbitrary power ('gold and blood' were the regular attributes of tyranny for Shelley). Such laws *tempt and slay* through *agents provocateurs*, who induced men to rebel and then betrayed them to execution.

12. *Time's worst statute*: the worst piece of legislation still on the statute-book of Time is the legislative assembly itself, the unreformed Parliament.

13. *a glorious Phantom*: the Spirit of Liberty. Shelley's *Address to the People* (1817) shows that the wry stress on *may* was fully intended:

Let us follow the corpse of British Liberty slowly and reverentially to its tomb; and if some glorious Phantom should appear and make its throne of broken swords and sceptres and royal crowns trampled in the dust, let us say that the Spirit of Liberty has arisen from its grave and left all that was gross and mortal there, and kneel down and worship it as our Queen.

PAGE 112. AN EXHORTATION. The 'argument' of this little poem, written partly as 'a kind of excuse for Wordsworth' the turncoat, partly in self-mockery, is close-knit and witty. Just as chameleons are supposed to live on light, so poets live on love. But light makes chameleons change colour, while poets are only changeable when deprived of the love they crave for; and living 'on this cold earth' is, to a poet, like living in darkness to a chameleon. Yet if poets accepted worldly success instead of love, they too would become earth-bound. (Chameleons inhabit sunny Africa, and are tree-dwellers.)

PAGE 113. TO A SKYLARK. The skylark figures here as most ordinary people know it: as an invisible source of music. Hence it symbolizes the (Romantic) poet. But the poem is not as naïve as it may seem. The lark has all that a poet lacks—supreme fluency, profuseness, an audience—yet it only has these things because (being in elemental contact with Nature) it has an elemental purity of joy that cuts it off completely from humanity and poet alike.

5. Here, and in the two final stanzas, Shelley remembers Milton's picture of Adam and Eve before the Fall:

> in fit strains pronounc't or sung
> Unmeditated, such prompt eloquence
> Flowd from thir lips, in Prose or numerous Verse. . . .
> (*Paradise Lost*, v. 145–52)

6–8. *Higher still . . . fire: From the earth* goes with l. 1, not with *springest*: the lark, already airborne, mounts higher and higher, like a sunset cloud (suggesting also the 'cloud of fire' that springs from a volcano and rains down sparks).

22. *that silver sphere*: Venus, whose brilliant disk seems to shrink (*narrows*) as the sky lightens. 'Your shrill delight is as piercing as the rays of Venus (as sharp as Love's arrows).'

49. *aërial*: rhyming (roughly) with 'May-serial'.

96–100. *Better . . . ground*: to have the lark's powers would help a poet more than all his metrical resource or book-learning.

PAGE 117. THE CLOUD. A brilliant light exercise in imaginative and technical virtuosity, using chiefly monosyllables and a metre familiar to everyone in the nursery-rhyme 'Little Bo-Peep'; and an example of Shelley's myth-making powers. King-Hele (see Bibliography) has an excellent account of *The Cloud*, pp. 219–27.

15–16. *And all . . . blast*: A 'banner' cloud hangs motionless on the lee of a mountain-peak, while the wind blows round it on either side.

17–30. *Sublime . . . rains*: the cloud's electric charge (its *pilot*) is attracted by opposite charges underwater, and wherever the 'pilot' hovers, his electrical opposite (*the Spirit he loves*) follows beneath, till the potential between them is run off in rain. (It was then believed that clouds were guided by electricity.)

33. *rack*: high, wind-driven cloud.

58. *and these* refers audaciously to *stars* seven lines back, helped by the rhyme *bees* and by the reader's instinctive pairing of 'moon and stars'.

59–60. *burning zone . . . girdle of pearl*: solar halo and lunar halo: a ring round sun or moon formed by high-altitude clouds of ice-crystals.

71. *The sphere-fire above*: the sun.

79. *convex gleams*: rays of sunlight refracted by the curvature of the atmosphere.

84. *unbuild*: a daring paradox. When a cloud 'dies', its cenotaph or death-monument is an empty sky, a *blue dome of air*; so when the cloud reforms, the dome-cenotaph is 'unbuilt'—the empty sky fills up again with vapour.

PAGE 119. LETTER TO THE GISBORNES. This 'delightful and laughable and exquisite description in verse of our house and Henry's workroom', as Mrs. Gisborne called it, was written in Leghorn when the Shelleys were occupying the house of Maria and John Gisborne while their friends visited London. Maria Gisborne, an old friend of the Godwins, had nursed Mary Shelley after her mother died. Shelley's study was the workroom of Henry Reveley (Mrs. Gisborne's son by a former marriage), a nautical engineer. The letter was written to the three Gisbornes collectively, and was not meant for publication.

10–14. *a soft cell . . . immortality*: the whole image is of a silk-moth. When his caterpillar-form 'fades away', this cocoon of verse will allow the poet to emerge as a winged memory to be nourished for ever in the hearts of his friends.

19. *gin*: engine.

20. *figured spells*: magical calculations.

23. *Vulcan*: god of the smithy.

24. *Ixion* was bound to a wheel for trying to seduce Jupiter's wife Juno.

25. *St. Dominic*: founder of the Dominicans, who later conducted the Inquisition on the Continent.

27. *philanthropic council*: a sardonic reference to Philip II's council that planned the Catholic crusade against England in 1588. The grammatical structure is: 'who thought to pay interest . . . by giving a foretaste . . . with thumbscrews'.

33–34. *Spain . . . hearth*: '. . . Ferdinand has proclaimed the Constitution of 1812, and called the Cortes. The Inquisition is abolished, the dungeons opened and the patriots pouring out' (Mary Shelley to Maria Gisborne, 26 March 1820).

37. *storm-encompassed isles*: e.g. the Hebrides, where many Spanish ships (supposed to be carrying instruments of torture) were wrecked in 1588.

45. *Proteus*: the 'Old Man of the Sea' in the *Odyssey*, who changed into different things to escape his captor.

51. *Tubal Cain*: traditionally the first metal-worker (Genesis iv. 17–24).

53–54. *The elements . . . time*: the basic components of steamboats.

95. *Laplace*: French astronomer and mathematician (d. 1827). *Saunderson . . . Sims*: authors of old textbooks of geometry (Nicholas Saunderson) and of algebra (Robert Simson).

98. *Baron de Tott*: French diplomat whose *Mémoires sur les Turcs* (1784) had a European popularity.

106. *Archimage*: Archimago, wicked Enchanter in Spenser's *Faerie Queene*.

107–12. *devilish enginery . . . self-content*: Shelley jokingly describes his poetry in terms of one of Henry Reveley's steam-engines, just a devilish device for stirring up angry reviews—such as one he (wrongly) attributed to the Rev. Milman.

114. *Libeccio*: the south-west wind.

142. *the sad enchantress*: Memory (of l. 132).

155. *A shroud of talk*: grammatical subject of the infinitives *to hide*, *blame* (l. 158), *anatomize* (l. 160), and *guess* (l. 162). The original construction is resumed in l. 166.

164–5. *When . . . safe*: 'when we shall be as safe in death as we were before we were born'.

175. *wisest lady*: Maria Gisborne, who had been teaching Shelley Spanish by reading the plays of Calderon (d. 1681) with him. *indued*: 'clothed myself in.'

198. *fallen*: i.e. like Milton after the Restoration (*Paradise Lost*, VII. 25–26).

213. *Shout*: London statuary and cast-maker.

217. *learned*: one syllable.

233. *English Peacock*: T. L. Peacock, the comic novelist. This 'peacock' had just become a retiring bird by marrying a 'fair one' from Caernarvon, Jane Gryffydh, and taking a job at the India House.

240. *cameleopard*: strictly, a giraffe; but Shelley (who probably pronounced it 'camel-leopard') means the sort of 'pard' that drew the chariot of Bacchus, slyly implying that the marriage is of milk and wine. Peacock cultivated the pagan gods, and was fond of his bottle.

250. *Horace Smith*: a generous London friend, both stockbroker and witty poet.

272. *Pollonia*: Mary Shelley had teased Henry Reveley by pretending that Apollonia Ricci, daughter of their Leghorn landlord, was pining in his absence. This had been a playful fiction; the prostitute's love is a fiction, too, but a horrible one.

286. *contadino*: Italian peasant.

305. *syllabubs*: drinks made of cream and wine.

317. *Helicon*: mountain of the Muses. *Himeros*: 'a synonym of Love' (Shelley's note). He means: 'Then I shan't need to drug myself with composition or emotional distractions.'

PAGE 130. THE PURSUED AND THE PURSUER. In 1820 Shelley wrote incidental lyrics for two short verse plays by his wife. Ovid (*Met.* v. 577–641) tells how the river Alpheus, seeing Arethusa bathing, took human form and pursued her. Diana wrapped the girl in a mist, but in her terror she changed into a stream, whereupon Alpheus resumed his river-shape and mixed his waters with hers in an island near Sicily.

Mary Shelley used the romantic lines known as *Arethusa* in her play *Proserpine*, and probably never saw this delicately mocking second version, which presents the nymph as both vain and cold. It has no title in the draft.

PAGE 131. APOLLO SINGS. Mary Shelley's second play, *Midas*, opens with Pan challenging Apollo to a singing-match. Tmolus, and Midas king of Phrygia, are judges. Tmolus votes for Apollo, but Midas backs Pan, and the angry sun-god gives him asses' ears for his bad taste. Shelley wrote the lyrics for both competitors, suiting this to Apollo's 'golden lyre', the other to the 'blithe pipe' of Pan, and allowing them thirty-six lines each.

33–34. *All harmony . . . mine*: Apollo was also god of music, of prophecy, and of medicine.

PAGE 132. ADONAIS. Keats and Shelley were only acquaintances. Keats was inclined, Leigh Hunt wrote, 'to see in every man of birth a sort of natural enemy'; he did not think art and politics should mix, and refused (he said) to visit Shelley while writing *Endymion*, 'that I might have my own unfettered scope'. When told of his illness, Shelley invited him to Pisa; Keats accepted provisionally, but did not come; and it was two months after the event when indirect news arrived of his death, caused, it was said—ignoring Keats's actual tough-mindedness—by sensitivity to anonymous criticism. Shelley had no details, and assumed that the brief (and not unreasonable) disparagement of *Endymion* in the *Quarterly Review* for April 1818 was the guilty article. He told John Gisborne: 'I have dipped my pen in consuming fire for his destroyers, otherwise the style is calm and solemn.'

The emotional intensity of the poem, therefore, comes from sources other than personal friendship. First, Shelley was deeply impressed by *Hyperion*, and thought it the work of a great genius. Second, Keats was championed as representative of all poets, living and dead, who had suffered persecution from the enemies of the imagination, including Shelley himself, who 'in another's fate now wept his own'. Third, some of the poignancy in the poem was transferred to Keats from Shelley's three-year-old son William, buried in the same place two years earlier.

In *Adonais*, Keats's famous advice was taken to 'be more of an artist, and load every rift of your subject with ore'. It is the most slow-moving of the longer poems, 'a highly-wrought piece of *art*', which Shelley thought his 'least imperfect' poem. Its mountain shepherds and other *personae* are traditional to the pastoral elegy: there are many echoes from Moschus's elegy on the Greek poet Bion, and from Bion's own *Lament of Venus for Adonis*, lines from both of which Shelley had translated.

The myth. The name *Adonais* is an adaptation of *Adonis*. Venus loved a mortal, Adonis, who was killed by a boar. Her tears revived him; but he returns to life only in summer, sleeping on flowers the rest of the year, with Proserpine in the underworld. (See Spenser, *Faerie Queene*, III. vi. 29–49; Keats, *Endymion*, III. 387–533). This fertility-myth of a boy loved by a goddess, done to death by a savage beast, and sleeping or waking with the seasonal life of Nature, parallels the fate of Keats, a young poet loved by the Muse and killed by a Tory reviewer; whose body is reabsorbed into the vitality of Nature and whose spirit lives on with the 'enduring dead'.

Urania is Poetry itself ('great Poesy', in the draft). She corresponds to Venus in the myth, but is Adonais's 'mother', not lover; it is suggested, metaphorically, that Adonais (i.e. Keats's poetry) is the offspring of Milton and of the Heavenly Muse invoked by Milton as Urania in *Paradise Lost* (VII. 1–39); hence Urania's 'widowhood' since Milton's death (l. 47).

5. *obscure compeers*: fellow-Hours not honoured by selection.

11–12. *pierced . . . darkness*: wounded by anonymous attack (Psalms xci. 5–6).

14. *Paradise*: pleasure-garden or park.

15. *one*: i.e. one Echo, who repeated Keats's poetry.

29. *He*: Milton, who died in 1674 amid the triumph of all he had fought against (*pride* is the object of *Trampled and mocked*). Times are much the same, it is implied.

36. *the third*: the third epic poet, after Homer and Dante.

39–43. *And happier . . . prime*: Minor poets whose work survives might well have counted themselves lucky compared with major poets whose writings have been destroyed. *refulgent prime*: full powers.

48–49. *Like a pale . . . dew*: a precise compliment to Keats: Urania's grief over Adonais is like Isabella's over her 'pot of basil' (which contained her murdered lover's head).

51. *extreme*: latest of all.

55. *that high Capital*: Rome.

60. *still*: yet.

67–68. *Invisible . . . dwelling-place*: decomposition (the *eternal Hunger* of l. 69) waits to show his body how to achieve its final transformation.

88. 'She' (l. 89) is the Lost Angel, Adonais's brain the Paradise.

94. *anadem*: head-band.

96–99. *would break . . . cheek*: 'was ready to break her bow and arrows, as if to check the pain of a great loss by incurring a small loss; and was even ready to deaden the fire of love's arrows against his cold face'.

100. *Splendour*: Dream, poetic imagining.

101–3. *That mouth . . . beneath*: the mouth that could put the Dream into words, enabling it to reach the hearer's emotions through his rational consciousness.

107. *clips*: embraces.

120–3. *Morning . . . day*: Dawn's unbound hair (a mark of mourning), forming rainclouds instead of dew, hid the last stars of night (*the aërial eyes that kindle day*).

133–4. *those . . . sounds*: the lips of Narcissus, who scorned Echo's love.

134–5. *a drear . . . hear*: Echo will not echo the woodmen's songs; she is busy murmuring Keats's poetry to herself (l. 128).

140–1. *Phoebus . . . Narcissus*: Hyacinth was a boy Phoebus (Apollo) loved, but accidentally killed. Narcissus was made to love his own reflection, as a punishment for scorning Echo.

144. *odour . . . ruth*: the hyacinth and narcissus (now thought of as flowers) breathe sighs of pity instead of perfume.

145. *Thy spirit's sister*: so called because Keats wrote the *Ode to a Nightingale*.

147–51. *Not so . . . thee*: the logical order is: *the eagle . . . doth . . . not so . . . complain . . . as Albion wails . . . . scale Heaven*: i.e. by writing about the sun-god Hyperion.

160. *brere*: bush (=briar).

169. *All baser things*: i.e. things less heavenly than the stars.

174–5. *Like incarnations . . . death*: star-shaped flowers, using perfume instead of radiance, 'light up' the darkness of death.

177. *that . . . knows*: the mind (also *the intense atom*, l. 179).

179. *sightless*: invisibly swift.

187–9. *As long . . . sorrow*: time and change are the price we must pay for the beauty of earth's colours (see stanza LII).

195. *their sister*: the Echo who repeated Keats's poems in l. 15.

204–6. *So*: 'in just such a way'.

204. *rapt*: carried away.

219. *Blushed to annihilation*: 'white Death' contradicts (and so annihilates) himself if he blushes.

227. *so long but as*: only for as long as.

228. *heartless*: i.e. broken-hearted.

234. *I . . . Time*: Urania is the mother of mortal poets, so her own immortality only binds her for ever to the world of change.

236. *trodden . . . men*: conventional ways of thinking and writing.

238. *the unpastured dragon*: the monster of convention, hungry for victims.

240. *the mirrored shield*: such as Perseus used against the Medusa.

250. *The Pythian of the age*: Byron who, as Apollo killed the dragon Python, disposed of the critics in *English Bards and Scotch Reviewers*, and afterwards had nothing but flattery from them.

Stanza XXIX. A great poet, like the sun, generates a lot of parasitic life, snakes and mayflies; he uncovers the truth, as the sun scatters mist (*Making earth bare*); he outshines lesser poets as the sun hides the stars (*veiling heaven*). When he dies, all who made a living by attacking or imitating him (*the swarms that dimmed or shared* his light) die off too, and his lesser fellow poets can be seen shining again, like stars after sunset.

262. *mountain shepherds*: other poets.

264. *Pilgrim of Eternity*: Byron, eternally famous for *Childe Harold's Pilgrimage*.

268–9. *from . . . wrong*: Thomas Moore, Irish poet who had fiercely attacked English policy in Ireland (*Ierne*).

271. *Midst . . . note*: 'among the smaller fry'. The *frail form* is Shelley's own.

276. *Actaeon*: was turned into a stag for seeing Artemis (Diana) naked, and his own hounds tore him to pieces.

280. *pardlike*: i.e. like the leopards that drew the chariot of Bacchus.

283. Stressed: *The weíght of the súperíncúmbent hóur.*

Stanza XXXIII. Shelley appears as a Bacchante (see Appendix B), carrying the thyrsus, or ivy-wreathed spear tipped with a pine-cone, a fertility-symbol (but this cone is of cypress, for mourning). Violets and pansies (pensées) are associated with memory.

298. *partial moan*: biassed lament.

300. *Who*: who it was who.

301. 'As if in a foreign language' to Urania, who only recognizes genuine poets—he is a failure.

305–6. *Made bare . . . so!* Cain had been branded with the same infamy as Christ—oh, that so little distinction should be made between the worst and the best of men! (Shelley is not claiming to be either, but is saying that his own infamy is meaningless, because attached without discrimination.)

307. *What softer voice*: Leigh Hunt's.

317. *deaf and viperous murderer*: Psalms lviii. 4.

319. *nameless*: anonymous.

320–3. *It felt . . . song*: Keats's 'prelude' (*Endymion*) silenced the envy, &c., of all hearers except the reviewer.

328. *But be thyself*: 'simply be what you are'.

329. *at thy season*: every quarter—when the *Review* appeared.

334. *our delight*: Adonais.

367. *scarf*: mist or cloud.

381. *plastic stress*: shaping force.

384–5. *Torturing . . . bear*: forcing the stubborn material to resemble the 'one Spirit' as nearly as each particular object will allow.

388. Human 'stars' in the sky of history.

395. *the dead live there*: creative minds of the past are a living influence on young thinkers.

397. *inheritors . . . renown*: those dying before maturity. Chatterton (to whom Keats dedicated *Endymion*) committed suicide at 17; Sir Philip Sidney died a heroic death at 32; Lucan, Roman poet who conspired against Nero but broke under interrogation, vindicated himself by his manner of suicide, at 26.

414. *Vesper*: the Evening Star (Hesperus). This image links the poem's closing lines to the Greek epigram at the beginning:

> Thou wert the morning star among the living,
>   Ere thy fair light had fled—
> Now, having died, thou art as Hesperus, giving
>   New splendour to the dead.
>
>   (Plato: Shelley's translation)

Stanzas XLVII–XLVIII. 'It is foolish (*fond*) to mourn for Adonais, when Totality is so immense compared with our ignorant littleness; so don't worry too much, in case, when death is near, you feel you have built too much hope on an afterlife. In any case' (the next stanza continues), 'Adonais is immortal in the same sense as earlier "kings of thought".'

428–9. *For such . . . prey*: men like Keats derive no glory from lying among the ruins of Rome, which are monuments of greed and oppression, but add glory to those ruins.

439–55. *a slope . . . thou!*
The English burying place is a green slope . . . under the pyramidal tomb of Cestius, and is, I think, the most beautiful and solemn cemetery I ever beheld. To see the sun shining on its bright grass . . . and hear the whispering of the wind among the leaves of the trees which have overgrown the tomb of Cestius, and the soil which is stirring in the sun warm earth, and to mark the tombs, mostly of women and young people who were buried there, one might, if one were to die, desire the sleep they seem to sleep. (Shelley to Peacock, 22 December 1818.)
Shelley's son William is remembered in ll. 440, 453–5. Gaius Cestius was an obscure Roman tribune.

460. The Unity pervading all earthly things is eternal; the things themselves are transient.

Stanza LII. Just as white sunlight shining through stained glass separates into many colours, so the eternal Unity breaks up into the many lives and objects of earthly existence. Colour, though beautiful, 'stains' white light; death shatters our separate lives, but reunites us with 'the One'. All the beauty and art of ancient Rome is inadequate to convey this Total glory embodied in it.

470. *are gone before*: 'are dead already'.

Stanza LIV. The eternal Beauty, though dimmed by birth into earthly existence, shines on through all earthly things according to how closely they resemble that Beauty (the reckless plural verb and mixed metaphor reinforce the paradox).

489–90. *the trembling . . . given*: those who have never dared submit themselves to the driving force of the imagination. The two final stanzas do not mean 'I am dying', but 'I am inspired'.

PAGE 151. THE AZIOLA. The Scops Owl, a small bird with a single monotonous cry, whose Italian name is really 'assiolo'. The poem was evidently unfinished, and Mary Shelley may have changed the last word so as to make a rhyme.

7–9. *how elate . . . hate*! Shelley describes in advance his relief at being told it was only an owl.

PAGE 152 TWO CHORUSES FROM HELLAS. *Hellas* (the title, 'Greece', was suggested by Edward Williams) celebrates the Greek rebellion against Turkish rule, news of which came on 1 April 1821. Shelley's model, Aeschylus's play *The Persians*, imagines how news of the Greek victory of Salamis was received at the court of the defeated Persians; similarly, *Hellas* imagines reports of this new struggle for freedom reaching the Turkish Sultan as his empire begins to collapse. But information was so scanty that only parts of the poem are more than 'a mere improvise', as Shelley called it.

Shelley feared—mistakenly—that England might support Turkey against the Greeks, and crush the revolt. Hence 'the final chorus is indistinct and obscure', like the events it foreshadows (Shelley's note). This Chorus is the sequel to the first, which comes near the beginning of the play; each has forty-two lines. The speakers, Greek slaves, stand for Christianity against the Mohammedan oppressor, but their deeper hope is for a society that will supersede both religions (see Chorus II, ll. 5–6). Shelley was passionately aware of what civilization owed to Greek democracy. 'We are all Greeks,' he wrote in the Preface.

CHORUS I

5. *But they . . . immortal*: material worlds are continually disintegrating, while human minds undergo reincarnation (Shelley's note explains that this is poetic conjecture, not a statement of belief). *still*: ever (also in l. 11).

9. *brief . . . light*: thinking beings, 'to use a common and inadequate metaphor, *clothe themselves in matter*' (Shelley's note).

13–14. *Bright . . . cast*: their stage of perfection depends on what they did with their last lives and with the institutions they last inherited.

15. *A Power*: Jesus Christ.

25–28. *The moon . . . on*: Mohammed lived six centuries after Christ, but the religion he founded (its emblem is a crescent moon) will die before Christianity.

Stanza III. Christianity represents 'Truth' compared with the dream-world of the ancient gods, but error compared with the 'golden years' to come—a source of bloodshed and suffering (*turned*, in l. 41, is a participle). This is a 'revision' of Milton's *Hymn on the Morning of Christ's Nativity*, whose metre it imitates.

CHORUS II

4. *weeds*: garments (as in 'widow's weeds').

9. *Peneus*: river watering the beautiful Vale of Tempe (Lykostomo).

12. *Cyclads*: islands of the Greek archipelago.

13. *Argo*: ship in which Jason recovered the Golden Fleece.

18. *Calypso*: goddess who kept Ulysses from going home for seven years.

19–20. *O, write . . . be!* 'Let us have no more *Iliads*, if more wars are needed to furnish subjects for them.'

21–24. *Nor mix . . . knew*: Laius, king of Thebes, was the father of Oedipus (see note to *P.U.* I. 346–7, p. 194). Perhaps: 'Don't corrupt your new freedom with hatred and revenge, no matter what terrible problems may face you in the future.'

31. *Saturn and Love*: 'deities of a real or imaginary state of innocence and happiness' (Shelley's note), before Jupiter's usurpation ended the Age of Gold.

33. *all who fell*: 'the Gods of Greece, Asia, and Egypt', superseded by Jesus Christ (*One who rose*).

34. *many unsubdued*: 'the monstrous objects of the idolatry of China, India,' &c., not yet discredited.

40. *bitter prophecy*: i.e. of renewed bloodshed, in Virgil's Fourth Eclogue:

'. . . the rule of Saturn is restored . . . all traces that remain of our iniquity will be effaced and, as they vanish, free the world from its long night of horror. . . . Even so, faint traces of our former wickedness will linger on. . . . Wars even will repeat themselves and the great Achilles be despatched to Troy once more.'[1]

42. i.e. if the earth is *never* to achieve peace, it might as well perish.

PAGE 155. TO JANE. THE INVITATION. Shelley was strongly attracted to Jane Williams, and this poem (given her with a sequel, *To Jane. The Recollection*) celebrates a walk he took with her and Mary Shelley through the pinewoods to the sea near Pisa, on 2 February 1822.

9. *halcyon*: calm and blue. The halcyon (kingfisher) was supposed to build a nest on the sea in midwinter, and to ensure calm weather ('halcyon days') while she brooded her eggs.

38. *Death . . . stave*: 'I'll listen to your poetry when I'm dead' (*stave*: stanza).

64. *us*: stressed (to contrast with *deep east*).

PAGE 157. THE TRIUMPH OF LIFE. Shelley left his last powerful, though difficult, long poem in rough draft when he died. Yet its formal beauty is impressive, and this harsh, disenchanted vision of life, ordered into perfectly-controlled *terza rima*, has appealed strongly to modern readers. Petrarch's *Triumph of Death* and *Triumph of Love*, besides Dante's *Divine Comedy*, suggested some of the details and atmosphere, but it is very different from these poems in content. The first 215 of its 547 completed lines are given here.

Plan. The Narrator, resting under a hillside, 'remembers' having been there before. He then sees a Chariot like one used in a Roman 'Triumph' when the victor paraded his conquered enemies before the exulting people. One of its ex-followers, Rousseau, now describes how *he*

[1] *Virgil: the Pastoral Poems*, trans. E. V. Rieu, Penguin Classics, 1949, pp. 41–42.

awoke under a hillside, and how, after deserting a 'fair Shape' that first appeared to him, in order to join the celebrants of this same Chariot of 'Life', he ended up disfigured and broken. The poem, which is probably almost complete, breaks off just as the Narrator and Rousseau begin to discuss the meaning of the vision they have shared.

The plan of the poem depends on a close parallel between the Narrator's life-experience and Rousseau's. Rousseau, a writer and thinker greatly admired by Shelley, had taught that 'Man is born free, and everywhere he is in chains', and had recommended simplicity of life in harmony with Nature, but he himself had plunged into fashionable life at the age of 28 (nearly Shelley's age in 1822), and eventually died a paranoiac. In the poem, Rousseau's awakening under the hill symbolizes his birth (as in Wordsworth's *Immortality Ode*: 'Our birth is but a sleep and a forgetting', &c.); and the 'fair Shape' embodies the early ideals he abandoned. Thus what the Narrator 'remembers' (ll. 33–39) is his own birth, and the Chariot of 'Life' offers him a similar temptation to that which had destroyed Rousseau. Shelley's moral integrity was threatened by his involvement with Jane Williams; and he was disillusioned with politics, foreseeing that the coming contest in England over Reform, far from creating a genuine new society, would be one of 'gold and blood' on both sides—a mere Party struggle.

But this foresight only intensified Shelley's belief in 'what ought to be': *The Triumph of Life* is his last and greatest attack on what he thought life-denying in existing society. The poem sets the order of natural law, the homage of all creation to the purposeful sun (ll. 1–20), against false 'Life'—the monstrous, aimless distortions of a civilization based on self-interest. The career of 'Life's' Chariot symbolizes the blind onrush of existing society through the present moment, unwilled and directionless, dragging with it an ever-growing legacy of error and weakness from the past (those bound to the Chariot), and worshipped by the self-deluding opportunism of the living (the dancers). Those enslaved by 'Life' are the famous dead: men who (like Napoleon) openly sought their own ends, and men who (like Plato, or Rousseau himself) opposed 'Life' but were overcome through some failure of personal integrity. All but a 'sacred few' (such as Jesus and Socrates) are opportunists, turning away from true harmony with Nature for the sake of illusory power or pleasure; and all are rewarded in the end by death. The title, *The Triumph of Life*, might be paraphrased as 'The victory-parade of Death-in-life'.

7. *orison*: prayer.

12. *orient*: rising (with connotations of Eastern richness). The sun 'lights' the flowers and releases their perfumes.

23. *cone of night*: the shape of the earth's shadow in space.

26. *green Apennine*: the Apennine hills skirt the sea round the Gulf of Genoa.

61. *affliction . . . breath*: their tortured breathing as they run.

78. incomplete in the draft.

79–85. *Like . . . chair*: the 'old moon in the new moon's arms', a sign of coming storm.

94. *Janus-visaged*: Janus was a two- or four-faced Roman god who presided over new undertakings, including business; hence the ironical pun on *profit* (l. 100).

103. *banded eyes*: unused potentialities of science and imagination.

115. incomplete in the draft.

121–2. *all who . . . suffering*: perhaps: 'all who are demoralized in their old age by misery either suffered or inflicted on others'.

126. *the great winter*: the end of the world.

131. *native noon*: eagles traditionally lived near the blazing sun.

134. *they . . . Jerusalem*: Socrates (perhaps with other Athenians), and Jesus.

145. *that fierce Spirit*: sexual passion. Shelley disapproved of both sensuality and chastity as ends in themselves.

157–8. *the fiery . . . snaps*: the tension holding each as an individual apart, like an electric potential between two charged clouds, is broken down in sexual union.

160. *nor . . . single*: i.e. they die in couples.

172. *round them*: i.e. round the interposing shadows.

175. cold impotence destroys the old, hot sensuality the young.

190. *Feature*: Form, Shape (Lat. *factura*).

204. *Rousseau*: Jean-Jacques Rousseau (d. 1778). Genevese writer and reformer, a powerful influence during and after the French Revolution (ll. 206–7).

210. *wreaths of light*: not saintly haloes but emblems of intellectual supremacy.

212. *to know themselves*: 'Know thyself', a Socratic motto, was inscribed over the temple of Apollo at Delphi.

214–15. *And for the morn . . . evening*: 'instead of the enlightenment they professed to bring, they themselves were engulfed in error before they died'.

PAGE 165. LINES WRITTEN IN THE BAY OF LERICI. Probably Shelley's last lyric, about Jane Williams. The title is a later editor's.

1–6. The moon which is first addressed directly becomes a mere impersonal object after the comparison with Jane in l. 6.

8–14. *When . . . west*: the new moon (*Bright wanderer*), having climbed the *azure dome* of the day sky, is now, after dark, hovering just above the sea before setting into it. An albatross has long narrow wings like a crescent moon, and was said to sleep on the wing.

55–end. The fish, in choosing *Life* (active enjoyment) rather than *peace* (mere placid existence), are happy because the pleasure they seek blinds them to the price they will pay for it. But *Too happy* cuts both ways, meaning 'fatally happy' as well as 'enviably happy'.

57 was left unfinished.

PAGE 168. From: A DEFENCE OF POETRY. In January 1821 Shelley read an article by his friend Peacock in *Ollier's Literary Miscellany*, called *The Four Ages of Poetry*, which provoked him into writing a reply. Peacock had mockingly distinguished four ages in English poetry to correspond with the ages of iron, gold, silver, and brass in classical poetry: medieval barbarism, Shakespearian perfection, Augustan refinement, and a contemporary return to barbarism. 'Poetry was the mental rattle that awakened the attention of intellect in the infancy of civil society: but for the maturity of mind to make a serious business of the playthings of its childhood, is as absurd as for a full-grown man to rub his gums with coral, and cry to be charmed to sleep by the jingle of silver bells.' Adult modern intellects should apply themselves to the 'promotion of permanently useful ends and aims', such as chemistry, ethics, and political economy.

Peacock, a deft satirical poet himself, liked these utilitarian pursuits as little as he liked Romantic rhymesters, and was being ironical at the expense of both. But behind the double irony Shelley saw how plausible the utilitarian attack on poetry was, and drawing for support on Plato's *Ion* and Sir Philip Sidney's *An Apologie for Poetrie*, countered it by a passionately serious appeal to the Imagination as the source of all intellectual and moral progress. A second part in more specific defence of contemporary poetry was to have followed, but was never written.

Part I, of which about half is selected here, was finished by 12 March 1821, but remained unpublished until 1840.

ll. 27–36. *Every man . . . of the word*: in primitive society all are so naturally good at dance, song, poetry, and representational art that only the supremely talented can be distinguished; these are poets in the broad sense of the word.

ll. 40–48. *Their language . . . intercourse*: e.g. a living metaphorical language hardened into stock diction in eighteenth-century English poetry and was created anew by the metaphors of the Romantics.

l. 73. *the one*: the eternal Unity of which 'time and place and number' are fragments (see *Adonais*, LII).

l. 77. *that imperial faculty*: the imagination.

ll. 84–89. *For language . . . expression*: poetic language springs direct from the imagination, whereas, e.g. musical instruments interpose between the imagination and musical sound.

ll. 92–93. *The distinction . . . error*: '. . . it is not ryming and versing, that maketh Poesie. One may bee a Poet without versing, and a versifier without Poetry.' (Sidney, *An Apologie for Poetrie*).

ll. 95–96. *the permanent analogy of things*: the correspondence, revealed in metaphors, between natural law and human society (see Appendix A).

l. 112. *the Creator*: the poet.

l. 169. *considers*: 'treats'; i.e. this is not necessarily conscious on the poet's part, though Shelley presents it as if it were.

l. 234. *Riphaeus*: Dante put 'the one man among the Trojans most just' in the Christian Heaven, although he had died a pagan (*Paradiso*, xx. 67–69).

ll. 311–12. *mechanist*: machine-maker. *combines labour*: organizes the specialization of labour.

ll. 317–19. '*To him . . . away*': Mark iv. 25.

l. 321. *Scylla and Charybdis*: the two fatal sides of the Straits of Messina.

ll. 338–9. '*It is better . . . mirth*': Ecclesiastes vii. 2.

ll. 356–7. '*I dare not . . . adage*': *Macbeth* I. vii. 44–45.

l. 385. *scions*: shoots.

l. 416. *artificial*: skilful, artistic.

l. 422. '*unpremeditated song*': *Paradise Lost*, IX. 21–26.

l. 424. *Orlando Furioso*: Italian epic poem (1516) by Ariosto.

l. 453. *all that they combine*: i.e. all the elements of their poetry.

l. 460. *interlunations*: moonless periods. Shelley associated the moon with the cold light of reason. Hence: 'Poetry catches fleeting visions of the divine which only appear when the rational mind is not active, perpetuates them in art, and sends them out to meet the similar impressions (*their sisters*) in men who cannot express what they feel.'

ll. 480–1. '*The mind . . . heaven*': *Paradise Lost*, I. 254–5.

ll. 483–5. *And whether . . . things*: whether poetry creates its own world of fancy, or reveals the eternal reality underlying the existing world.

ll. 495–6. *Non merita . . . Poeta*: 'None deserves the name of creator except God and the Poet.' Tasso, Italian epic poet, wrote *Jerusalem Delivered* (1575).

l. 501. *institutor*: teacher.

ll. 515–16. '*there sitting . . . soar*': *Paradise Lost*, IV. 829.

l. 550. *obnoxious*: vulnerable.

ll. 582–3. *hierophants of an unapprehended inspiration*: servants of an unconscious influence.

l. 588. *unacknowledged legislators*: an expression adapted from Imlac's precept in Samuel Johnson's *Rasselas*, ch. X, that a poet should write 'as the interpreter of nature, and the legislator of mankind'.

DATE DUE